Bread? or Crumbs?

Bread? Or Crumbs?

A Collection of Sermons for Advent, Christmas, Epiphany, and Pentecost

REUBEN J. SWANSON

Wipf & Stock
PUBLISHERS
Eugene, Oregon

BREAD? OR CRUMBS?
A Collection of Sermons for Advent, Christmas, Epiphany, and Pentecost

Copyright © 2007 Reuben J. Swanson. All rights reserved. Except for brief quotations in critical publications or reviews, no part of this book may be reproduced in any manner without prior written permission from the publisher. Write: Permissions, Wipf & Stock, 199 W. 8th Ave., Eugene, OR 97401.

ISBN 10: 1-55635-194-1
ISBN 13: 978-1-55635-194-5

All Scripture quotations are taken from the *New Revised Standard Version Bible*, copyright © 1989, Division of Christian Education of the National Council of the Churches of Christ in the United States of America. Used by permission. All rights reserved.

Manufactured in the U.S.A.

*To
the many parishioners
in
Minnesota,
Illinois,
California,
Michigan,
Connecticut,
Iowa,
North Carolina,
and Ohio,
who have helped me to develop
the content
and the delivery
of the message.*

Contents

Preface / ix

1. Bread? or Crumbs? / 1
   The Sixteenth Sunday after Pentecost—Mark 7.24–30
2. Noah and the Ark / 13
   The First Sunday in Advent—Matthew 24.37–44
3. The Leafing Fig Tree / 29
   The First Sunday in Advent—Luke 21.29–33
4. The Axe, the Tree, and the Fire / 43
   The Second Sunday in Advent—Matthew 3.1–12
5. Light and Darkness / 55
   The Third Sunday in Advent—John 1.6–8
6. Consider the Candle / 71
   The Fourth Sunday in Advent—Matthew 1.18–25
7. No Room in the Inn / 85
   Christmas Eve, 1983—Luke 2.1–7
8. The Weeping Rachel / 99
   The Sunday after Christmas—Matthew 2.13–18
9. The Lamb of God / 113
   The Epiphany of Our Lord—John 1.29–34
10. The Opening Heavens / 127
    The First Sunday after the Epiphany—Mark 1.4–11
11. From Water to Wine / 141
    The Second Sunday after the Epiphany—John 2.1–11
12. In the Power of the Spirit / 155
    The Third Sunday after the Epiphany—Luke 4.14–21
13. Blessed are the Pure in Heart / 171
    The Fourth Sunday after the Epiphany—Matthew 5.1–10
14. The Dot and the Iota / 185
    The Fifth Sunday after the Epiphany—Matthew 5.17–20
15. Blessings and Woes / 199
    The Sixth Sunday after the Epiphany—Luke 6.20–26

16 The Sun and the Rain / 217
        The Seventh Sunday after the Epiphany—Matthew 5.38–48
17 Three Booths, a Cloud, and a Voice / 233
        The Day of the Transfiguration of Our Lord—Matthew 17.1–9
18 The Glory of God / 249
        The Tenth Sunday after Pentecost—Psalm 19.1
19 Not a Sparrow Will Fall / 261
        The Fifth Sunday after Pentecost—Matthew 10.26–31
20 Peace or a Sword? / 275
        The Sixth Sunday after Pentecost—Matthew 10.34–39
21 Where to Find Bread? / 289
        The Tenth Sunday after Pentecost—John 6.1–15
22 A Journey into Faith / 303
        The Fifteenth Sunday after Pentecost—Matthew 19.10–12
23 Treasure and the Heart / 313
        Matthew 6.19–21
24 Friend, Go Up Higher! / 325
        Luke 14.7–11
25 Speak the Word! / 335
        Luke 7.1–10
26 A Man Had Died / 341
        Luke 7.11–17
27 The Least and the Greater / 349
        Matthew 11.2–19
28 The Alabaster Flask / 357
        Luke 7.36–50

Preface

THE YEAR of our Lord, 1938, was a decisive year in my journey to faith. I was born into a home where my mother was a very devoted and faithful Christian, a member of the Lutheran Church. My father was not a church member, although he had been reared in a home where his mother, a Swedish Methodist, was a very pious and devoted believer. They were both children of immigrants from Sweden, although mother's entry into the world colored her outlook and viewpoint quite seriously since she was an illegitimate child. This was a cause for shame in that period of history. Mother's grandfather, the Rev. L. P. Stenstrom, was one of the pioneer Swedish Lutheran pastors in Northwest Minnesota. He served the Central Lutheran Church, a rural congregation at Pelican Rapids, the parish where I received my early church training, from 1880 to 1919. He was my baptismal pastor. Grandpa Stenstrom also served parishes at Elizabeth (forty years), Fergus Falls (twelve years), and Amor (twelve years). I have very pleasant memories of my great grandparents, for we lived with them for almost a year when my parents moved to Minnesota from North Dakota in 1921.

Mother came to a very profound religious commitment when working in Minneapolis as a young lady. She had been deeply troubled by fears and anxieties about her spiritual life, probably because of her birth. She lived with a very committed family of Pentecostals, "holy rollers" as they were called in those days, and attended their worship services. Here she received the gift of freedom from her fears and anxieties about her spiritual condition. The Pentecostals said that she should become one of them, since they had been instrumental in her receiving freedom from her fears and sense of guilt. Mother's response, "I am deeply grateful for what I have received, but I am returning to my Lutheran Church to bring to my church what I have received." Mother was faithful to that commitment throughout her lifetime. Our membership in Central Lutheran began in 1923 when Dad and Mother moved to the farm that had been mother's other grandparents, the Carl Larsons. They had given the land for the building of the church in 1880. Thus we were living very close to what became my spiritual home, the church where I was confirmed. All services, even the Sunday Church School, were in the Swedish language at the time. The first introduction to English was the Sunday School, for mother refused to send me and my brother since we were Americans and should use

Preface

English. Mother had the distinction of teaching the first English Adult Bible Class at the church in the mid twenties.

It was mother's custom to gather her brood together in the evening for the reading of the Bible and for prayer. Dad was never a part of our group. He was very strict about working on Sundays, doing only the necessary farm chores, but there was no participation in church worship or activities. One of the decisive events in my journey to faith was the evening Dad came into our gathering, took the Bible from Mother, read and prayed. Her faithfulness and her prayers had finally resulted in this wonderful change. I was about ten years of age when this change took place. Dad continued to be a faithful member of the Lutheran Church throughout his long lifetime, even to delivering the sermon when the pastor was away.

Confirmation, a week before my twelfth birthday, was a very important event on my journey to faith. We studied for a year with our pastor, memorizing Luther's Small Catechism and its explanation as well as many Bible verses. This has always been of great value to me in the parish and teaching ministry. We were given a Bible at the time of confirmation, and I set about religiously to read it in its entirety. I had very strong thoughts about becoming a missionary to China at that time of life. Alas! I went through the usual cycle of teenager denial, when we accommodate our religious convictions to conform to peer pressure. Not that I was terribly wicked. I did not smoke, or drink, or conform to some of the practices of youngsters seeking to express their independence from parental control. I was active in the youth activities of the church, sang in the choir, attended the youth Bible study group, but there was not that deep commitment at this time in my life to become a missionary or a church worker.

I graduated from high school at age sixteen with no prospects of continuing my education. Our country was in the midst of a critical depression and we also suffered from a severe drought. We were tenant farmers with plenty of food on the table but little money. Dad was compelled to sell out in 1937 because of ill health. I became an itinerant farm laborer and finally a grocery clerk. It was at this time a young lady friend suggested that I go to college. "You can work your way through. Others have done it." That was the very day for enrollment at Gustavus Adolphus College for the fall semester of 1938. I gave my employer a week's notice the next day, and then found to my dismay that I could not procure a loan at the bank. My girl friend's mother, a widow, came to my rescue, offering to sign a note at the bank. I had worked on her farm and had proven my capacities for honest and faithful stewardship. My college career began as a result, a week late, and on borrowed capital.

Preface

My enrollment in college was without any definite commitment to a particular career, although the idea of entering the ministry was always in my mind, suppressed by our innate tendency to be committed to our God but not too committed. I was not ready for bonds to be put upon my freedom to be and do what pleased me. My experience at Gustavus changed me in a radical way. I was exposed to young people who were genuinely committed to careers in the church. Through the guidance and counseling of some of the older students so committed, I came to the next great step on my journey to faith. It was the custom of our church, the Minnesota Conference of the Augustana Synod, to hold its Conference meeting on a week end in the springtime. Thus students from Gustavus went forth to conduct the Sunday services and preach the sermon on Conference Sunday. Although I felt completely inadequate, one of my senior mentors persuaded me to sign up. My first sermon was that spring of my freshman year at a small congregation at Kiester, Minnesota, and I have been preaching ever since.

One of our courses at Augustana Seminary at Rock Island, Illinois, was homiletics, the art of preaching. One of our assignments was to interview a pastor of our choosing on his style of preaching—preparation, content, delivery. My choice was John Helmer Olson, one of the first pastors ordained as a son of Central Lutheran, my home church. John Helmer was confirmed by my great grandfather Stenstrom and was the editor of our Church School paper for the older Sunday School children when I was a child. He had preached at Central when home on vacation and he was pastor of First Lutheran Church at St. Peter, Minnesota, when I was a student at Gustavus. He was a very gifted speaker, imaginative, and well versed in the Biblical texts for his sermons. The advice that stood out for me from the interview was, "Write your sermons for the first ten years of your ministry." This became my practice from the beginning of my ministry and continues to this day. Oscar Winfield, one of my college professors, said to me on one occasion when I had written a research paper for a course, "You write better than you speak." I said, "Everybody does." He replied, "No, it is the other way around."

Writing sermons became my practice. I took very seriously this role of the pastor. Most often in my career as a pastor, I have prepared sermons afresh. I have, however, rewritten and improved on sermons that I had previously given. An example is the title sermon in this anthology, "Bread? or Crumbs?" This was first prepared in 1950 early on in my pastorate at St. Paul's Lutheran, Ansonia, Connecticut. It was my farewell sermon when I moved from California to Ohio at the church of my membership, Mount

Preface

Cross Lutheran, Camarillo. This sermon, as all my sermons to the year 1976, was written in a prose format. The change to the poetic style came about in this way.

My dear wife of thirty-two years, Edna Carlson, died after a long and debilitating illness in 1975. She was my helpmeet and companion through two years of my seminary training and thirty years in the parish and teaching ministry. I then married a former college friend, Marian Mellgren, whom I had dated at Gustavus, a very gifted lady in the area of Speech and Debate. She was a teacher of English and Speech and Debate at the Amos Alonzo Stagg High School in Stockton, California, for many years. She coached the Speech and Debate teams and had the extraordinary record of placing thirteen of her students in the nationals in sixteen years. When we married and she came to North Carolina, I was professor at Western Carolina University. I also served a small Lutheran congregation at Andrews, North Carolina, fifty miles from home. The first time Marian heard me preach, she said, "That was poetic." In the succeeding weeks, she continued to remark about the poetic qualities of my sermons. Finally, I took one of my sermons, "I was there in Gethsemane," and typed it in the poetic format. It was as if I had written it that way in the beginning. This led to the publication of some of my sermons in a book entitled, "Roots Out of Dry Ground," in 1979.

I conclude by quoting the Preface to that book as written by Dr. John Bunn, Senior Minister, First Baptist Church, Sylva, North Carolina. I believe that he has expressed the uniqueness of my style in a very graphic way.

To read this anthology of the sermons by Reuben Swanson is to once again become acquainted with a venerable and highly imaginative homiletical structure. Rarely does an ancient homiletical form rise to newness of life and convince the reader of its validity for contemporary preaching. Yet, just such a sermonic device will confront every possessor of this volume. The author has subconsciously retrieved and modernized the dramatic method of prophetic poetic prose, which is one of the most exacting writing disciplines and of which the author is a past master. On the first reading, one acquainted with the Old Testament prophetic utterance, as found in newer English translations, will note a similarity of style, movement and emphasis. Dr. Swanson is to be commended for restoring to preaching this exciting mode of proclamation.

My utmost thanks and appreciation to my wife, Viola, also a former sweetheart before my college days who became my helpmeet and companion after the death of my dear Marian. She has been of invaluable help in preparing this volume for publication.

Sola Dei Gloria.

1

Bread? or Crumbs?

The Sixteenth Sunday after Pentecost

Mark 7.24–30

From there he set out and went away to the region of Tyre. He entered a house and did not want any one to know he was there. Yet he could not escape notice, but a woman whose little daughter had an unclean spirit immediately heard about him, and she came and bowed down at his feet. Now the woman was a Gentile, of Syrophoenician origin. She begged him to cast the demon out of her daughter. He said to her, "Let the children be fed first, for it is not fair to take the children's bread and throw it to the dogs." But she answered him, "Sir, even the dogs under the table eat the children's crumbs." Then he said to her, "For saying that, you may go—the demon has left your daughter." So she went home, found the child lying on the bed, and the demon gone.

Mount Cross Lutheran Church
Camarillo, California

Bread? or Crumbs?

Bread?
or crumbs?
What a strange woman in our gospel.
She longed for bread
when she could have crumbs.
We know this story was not written
in the twenty-first century.
Who eats bread today
when they can have crumbs?

Consider
the parable of the loaf.
A man was exceedingly hungry.
A loaf of bread was upon the table,
but he went to the cupboard
in search of crumbs.

A neighbor found him
a few days later beside the table.
The learned physician pronounced the cause
of his death malnutrition.
You see, the man had bread,
but he preferred crumbs.

The disciples asked their teacher
the meaning of the parable,
and he said,
"Behold,
the people of our day!
Lo, there is bread and to spare,
but they cry for crumbs.
Behold,
people starving, dying,
not for lack of bread,
but because they feed upon
a diet of crumbs."

The Bread of Life

Jesus said,
"I am the bread of life."
He never said,
"I am a crumb."
You and I have said to Jesus,
"You are not the bread of life.
You are a crumb."

If we truly believed
with all our heart
that Jesus is the bread of life,
he would be indispensable to us.
We would eat the loaf,
rather than nibble on the crumbs.
Do you believe he is the bread of life?
Why then is he not first
in your life?

The prodigal son
tried to live on crumbs,
very poor crumbs at that—
husks thrown to the swine.
When he came to himself,
When he realized how foolish to starve
when there was bread to eat,
he said,
"How many of my father's hired servants
have bread enough
and to spare,
while I perish here from hunger!
I will arise
and go to my father."

But tragedy of tragedies!
Many are not prodigals.
Many are seated in the front seats
of the table of the Lord,
who push back their chairs

Bread? or Crumbs?

famished and undernourished
because they did not eat bread,
but nibbled at the crumbs.

We are seated
at the table of the Lord.
The menu offers the bread of life.
Many of us are starved,
famished in our inner being.
As the starveling
stuffs himself with crumbs,
unaware that he is dying for lack of nourishment,
so we are too often
satisfied to stuff ourselves
upon substitutes and imitations
for the true bread of life.

And our souls have become
mean, dirty, shriveled, decaying hovels.
For souls
cannot become stately mansions
upon a diet of crumbs.

The carpenter
does not build a mansion
of hay, or stubble, or third-grade material.
Nor does the heavenly carpenter,
the Holy Spirit,
build of us an eternal temple
in which the living God
dwells,
unless we are nourished upon the best
that God offers
at his table—
the bread of life.

No Hunger

Jesus said,
"I am the bread of life;
he who comes to me shall not hunger."
Jesus is not a crumb!
He is bread!
The bread of life.
You and I have said,
"You are not bread.
You are a crumb!"

We eat bread
to satisfy our hunger,
to provide nourishment for our bodies,
to give strength
for our daily tasks.
In the same manner
Jesus is the bread of life
to satisfy our spiritual hunger,
to nourish our inner being,
to give us strength for daily service
in the kingdom of God.

Yet we are spiritually hungry;
many of us starving amidst plenty.
Bishop Hans Lilje
of Hannover,
visiting our churches in the United States said,
"The American people
are hollow inside."
We are hollow
because we have not truly eaten
of the bread of life.

Bread,
to satisfy our hunger,
must be eaten.
Bread must be digested
and assimilated into our bodies,

Bread? or Crumbs?

so that it becomes
the living cells of our flesh,
the red corpuscles of our blood.

If Jesus,
the bread of life,
is to satisfy our spiritual hunger,
he must be eaten;
that is, we must believe him;
we must receive him into our hearts and lives,
so that he becomes
the living cells of our soul,
the red corpuscles of our spirit.

Jesus
is the bread of life!
He offers himself to us
that we may never hunger.
He gives himself to us,
so that our spirits may be alert an active,
busy
with the business of the Lord.

He gives himself to us
so that our inner self may grow to be
healthy and strong,
alive and vital forever
through the creative power of God.

Why do we spend money
for that which is not bread?
Why do we starve our inner selves
by feeding upon crumbs?
There is no substitute for the bread of life!
All other bread—
pleasure, wealth, power,
honor, fame, piety,
religiosity, churchianity—
is subject to the decay of time.

Bread? or Crumbs?

The one who feeds
upon such crumbs
rather than upon the bread of life,
will starve and die.
Would we, like the prodigal, live upon crumbs?
Or will we like he,
awaken to the awareness, to the knowledge
how foolish to starve
when there is bread to eat?

Jesus offers himself,
the bread of life, to us.
Bread upon which living souls are nourished.
Bread from which big souls are shaped.
Souls alive and pulsing
with peace and joy,
with love and faith,
with kindness and meekness,
with humility and self-control.
Souls carved and shaped
by the heavenly builder
into the image and likeness
of Christ himself.

Bread For Our Children

What a difference
the food we eat.
What a tremendous difference between
nibbling on crumbs
and eating the bread of life.

If our nourishment
is only crumbs,
we will have lean, shallow, small souls.
What then do we bequeath
to our children
and to our children's children
but feeble,
infirm, shallow spiritual selves.

Bread? or Crumbs?

Jesus said,
"What father or mother among you,
if a child asks for bread,
will give the child a stone?"
Would we think of giving our child
a stone,
if the child begged for a piece of bread?

Too often we do precisely that
when our children look to us
for spiritual nourishment
and guidance.
We have not fed upon the bread of life.
We have not permitted the Holy Spirit of God,
the heavenly builder,
to fashion of our souls
stately mansions,
shaped in the image and likeness of Christ.

We remember
how old Mother Hubbard
went to the cupboard
to get her poor dog a bone.
When she got there
the cupboard was bare,
so the poor dog had none.
How often our spiritual cupboards
are as bare
as old Mother Hubbard's
when the children look to us for the bread of life.

Where is our faith?
Where are our works?
Our works of Christ-like love?
We are timid,
we are afraid,
to sacrifice and to give to our Lord
and to our neighbor
for fear

Bread? or Crumbs?

there will not be enough for ourselves.
Is it because our spiritual cupboards are bare?

Where is our commitment
to regular worship,
to Bible study,
to fellowship with believers,
to Christian conversation,
to an in-depth development of our spiritual being?

We have not learned
to trust God,
because we have not eaten fully,
we have not filled ourselves
upon the bread of life.

A diet of crumbs cannot produce
a great faith in God,
an undying love for him,
a serious concern for
the physical and spiritual welfare
of our children
and of our neighbor's children.

Only as Christ,
the living bread,
is received and eaten,
only as he is born in us through faith;
Only as he
becomes the dynamo, the powerhouse
empowering our lives,
can he fashion within us a great soul
of vision and imagination,
of courage and daring,
of faith, hope, and love.

Only as Christ lives in us
will we live and work and pray
unceasingly,
untiringly,
for the kingdom of God on earth.

Bread? or Crumbs?

To do this,
my sisters and brothers in Christ,
we must eat bread,
the living bread from heaven,
not just today,
but all our days on earth.

Bread?
or crumbs?

2

Noah and the Ark

The First Sunday in Advent

Matthew 24.37–44

As the days of Noah were, so will be the coming of the Son of man. For as in those days before the flood they were eating and drinking, marrying and given in marriage, until the day Noah entered the ark, and they knew nothing until the flood came and swept them all away, so too will be the coming of the Son of man. Then two will be in the field; one will be taken and one will be left. Two women will be grinding meal together; one will be taken and one will be left. Keep awake therefore for you do not know on what day your Lord is coming. But understand this: if the owner of the house had known in what hour of the night the thief was coming, he would have stayed awake and would not have let his house be broken into. Therefore you also must be ready, for the Son of man is coming at an unexpected hour.

Luther Memorial Church
Burbank, California

Noah and the Ark

Noah's ark,
an ancient myth
of the Mesopotamian world.
Evidently the myth was borrowed
by the Hebrew people
whose ancestors had lived in the area
in the time of Abraham
and perhaps earlier.

The myth
is the story of a man,
Noah,
who was righteous before God.
Noah built an ark
because he expected a great flood
upon the earth.

Is the myth true?
Evidently.
The story was known
by a number of people
who inhabited
the Mesopotamian region
in ancient times.

The flooding of
the two great rivers,
the Tigris and the Euphrates,
was a constant threat
before the people learned to control
the flow of water
by a series of dikes and canals.
Noah
lived before the time of the myth.

Later generations recalled
the time of
a catastrophic flood

that had devastated the valley
bringing death and destruction to many.

Noah's Ark

Noah
was a man
in touch with God.
He made preparations for a disaster
he believed was coming.
He built a large boat,
an ark.
He and his family,
a total of eight persons,
were saved from destruction
when that great flood occurred.

The myth
recalls that Noah's ark
landed on Mount Ararat
when the flood waters receded.
The ark
has been the object of search
in modern times.
Rumors persist
that the skeleton of an ancient boat
have been discovered
in the mountains of Ararat.

The rumors are probably false.
It is doubtful that a wooden ark
could have survived
the erosion and decay caused
by air, wind, and water,
and the changing temperatures.
It is doubtful that,
if any remains of an ark could be found,
that their identity
with this ancient Mesopotamian myth
and the Biblical account of

Noah
could be verified.

There are proof mongers
who seek authentic proof
to substantiate the truth
of Biblical stories.
There are those who need such proof
to believe in God.
The Scripture is not true in and of itself.
There must be tangible evidence—
the ark of Noah,
a shroud from Turin,
a piece of the cross upon which Christ died,
or the tomb in which his body was laid.

This is not the essence of faith.
The author of Hebrews writes,
"Faith is the assurance of things hoped for,
the conviction of things not seen."
Faith
is never grounded in proofs.
If it is, it is not faith.

Faith
is grounded only in the word
and promise of God.
Faith is trusting dependence
upon God
who is never visible to the human eye,
or present
to the touch of our hand.

The Warning

The reality of
Noah's ark,
or the existence of an ancient ark,
is not necessary for faith.
In the Biblical account

the ark
is a warning
to all who take God lightly,
to all who are indifferent to God,
to all who trust in themselves.
The message
of Noah's ark
is a call to be ready
at all times
for the coming of God.

The Gospel
always proclaims the presence of God.
The Gospel
always calls us to walk uprightly before him.
The Gospel
calls us to live the truth,
to live in faith and in love.
Death and destruction
are always at hand.
Tempest and flood,
earthquake and fire,
the powerful elements of nature
are always a threat
wherever we may live.

The threat
due to our mortality,
the very transient nature of life,
calls us
to make wise judgments
about how we live in this world.
We cannot stay the unceasing forces of nature,
mighty forces
bringing death and destruction
to the unwary,
to those who have not planned wisely
for tomorrow.

Noah and the Ark

What are the priorities
that govern and determine
the way we live?
In Noah's time
they were eating and drinking,
marrying and giving in marriage.
All necessary functions
to assure survival
for the human family.

We are always intent upon such vital functions:
eating and drinking,
marrying,
and giving in marriage.
But eating and drinking
and marriage
do not assure the survival
of the human race.

Tempest and flood are always with us,
earthquake and fire,
hurricane and tornado,
or even nuclear threat in our day
threatening
our survival.
We can never be certain
what the morrow will bring.
Unexpected death
is always our companion in life.

According to the myth,
the devastation
from the flood in Noah's time
was all but complete.
Only eight persons were saved.
There are priorities
more important than eating and drinking
or marrying.
The Gospel
always calls us to face up

Bread? or Crumbs?

to the highest priority of all,
to know God,
to trust him,
to do his will.

The Noah myth
is a warning
sounding forth from the pages of the ancient past
that the quality of life
is of far greater significance
for our survival
than eating and drinking,
or entering into the marriage covenant.

Noah
and his family were saved
because they heard the voice of God
and responded in faith.
The wickedness of humankind
was great upon the earth.
The stench
ascended even to the nostrils of God.
This dimension
of our story
sounds very modern.

What does God smell today?
Is there a sweet odor
ascending to heaven?
What of the murder of priests in El Salvador?
Or the murders
on the streets of Los Angeles?
Or the indulgence
in drugs,
alcohol,
sex,
and perversion in our own Burbank?

Noah and the Ark

We cannot,
and we will not
survive our own wickedness.
Evil is self-destructive.
Death and destruction
fall upon all
who do not heed God's call
to righteousness and holiness in
everyday life.
Upon all who go their own way,
who are indifferent to God,
to truth, justice,
righteousness, and godliness.

The Comparison

Noah's ark is important,
not as an archaeological find,
but as a lesson
to all who ignore God.
Jesus said,
"As were the days of Noah,
so will be the coming of the Son of man."

In Noah's day,
a torrential flood
swept away all who were not in communion with God.
Jesus said,
"In the day of the Son of man,
two men will be working in the field,
one will be taken
and the other left.
Two women will be grinding at the mill,
one will be taken
the other left."

We can say
in modern parlance,
two will be working in construction

Bread? or Crumbs?

in San Francisco.
A giant crane breaks loose and crashes upon them.
One was taken
and the other left.

We are always living
in our last days.
This moment is all we may call our own,
and this moment is immediately gone.
The future is not in our grasp.
We enter our future,
our tomorrow,
only by the grace of God.
Our God is the Lord of history.
Our God is the author of time.
Our time,
our life,
are in his hand.
We have here no abiding reality.

The finding of Noah's ark
cannot save us
from selfishness and greed,
from godlessness,
from our preoccupation with all that is fleeting
and fading.
God alone is our Savior.

The Gospel
is the power of God for salvation
to those who have faith;
this precious gift from God
is the hope for our future.
God's purpose in the time of Noah,
and God's purpose today is
to deliver us
from the destructive forces of sin,
from spiritual death,
from the powers of evil,
from all those enticements

Noah and the Ark

that would lead us
to devote our lives and our energies
to our own ends and ambitions.

God's purpose
according to the myth of Noah's ark is
to lead us to truth,
to the knowledge
that we cannot survive
apart from his saving grace.

There is destruction coming upon the earth.
We have tasted it
in hurricane Hugo
and the San Francisco earthquake.
Our lesson announces
that the end of the age is at hand.
Today, as always,
we are living in our last day.

What shall we do?
Shall we like Noah build an ark?
A safe refuge
in which we place our prized possessions?
Whatever is dear to us
in the hope that
life will continue into the future
in the same patterns
of security as our past?

Noah was saved by God
in order that a new beginning,
a new direction,
would distinguish the quality of human life on earth.
Only Noah
and his family
responded in faith to the warnings from God.
Though the destruction
was almost total,
the flood did not end the human family.

Bread? or Crumbs?

A new family of humanity
descended from Noah.
Nevertheless the flood
did not bring an end to sin and wickedness.

Noah was a righteous man,
but sin continued to abound.
In our own day,
history is a dismal tale
of man's inhumanity to man.
Human crimes
are more demonic,
more gross, more vile,
than the people of Noah's time could have imagined.
We cannot build an ark
large enough
to save us from our own self-destruction.

The word of God is
always both a warning
and a promise.
Watch!
You do not know when the Lord is coming.
Be prepared!
The Son of man is at hand.
Our salvation
is not an ark
that we may construct of earthly materials.
It is the ark of God
not shaped by human hands;
not a plan drawn by a human architect,
not a great ship constructed of earthly materials.

God alone is our Savior.
God saves
through the weak, frail hands
of one
who was one of us,
bone of our bone,
flesh of our flesh,

Noah and the Ark

blood of our blood.
One who became the victim
of man's spite and evil,
of man's inhumanity to man.

God saves
through that one who gave his life
for truth,
goodness, and love.
Through that one
whose priorities were the priorities of God.

The message of Advent
is a call
to put our house in order.
The highest priorities in life are not
eating and drinking,
marrying and giving in marriage.
Our highest priority is
to do the will of God.
The coming one is at the door.
The message today is,
Watch!
Be alert!
Be ready for the coming of the Lord!

Open wide the door
of your heart, your life, your mind,
says the messenger of God.
Be open
to the coming of the One who comes
from God
to abide in us
and to lead us in the pathways of God.

To be ready does not mean
to sit with folded hands and bated breath
waiting for the end
of this age,
waiting for the coming of the Son of man.

Bread? or Crumbs?

To be ready means
to do the work and the will of God today.

As Noah built an ark
before the coming of the flood,
So we are to plan and build and sow
the seed of the word of God
in the hearts and minds of people everywhere.
We are to share God's word of truth,
God's grace and love with all people
in the measure
we have received from our gracious and loving God.

We have the word of God,
the message of the cross,
the word of death to life;
a word powerful to deliver us,
not from tempest and flood,
not from hurricane and tornado,
but from all those forces of evil
that would destroy
our future,
our very life.
From all the forces that separate us from the living God.
The word and promise of God alone are
our salvation.

His word and promise
delivers us
from a far more terrible foe than flood or fire,
His word delivers
from those spiritual forces
that would destroy our innermost self,
our very being;
from all those forces that would forever end
our relationship to our Creator God.

The powerful word and promise of God
bring us to a focus
upon the true and eternal priorities of life

Noah and the Ark

in the world
and in the life to come—
faith, truth, love,
humility, goodness, and godliness.

Noah's ark is a powerful testimony
from our Creator and Savior God
that his purpose is
and has always been
to fashion all people everywhere into one community,
one family;
a family holy and true,
loving, and compassionate;
fathers and mothers,
sisters and brothers,
sons and daughters,
who demonstrate love and concern
for every other member of the human family on earth,
from the least to the greatest.

Only then can the myth of Noah's ark
come alive
in our hearts, our minds, our lives
as the salvation of the human race
from self-destruction,
from the terrible suffering and desecration we inflict
upon creation
and upon one another.

Hallelujah!
God's message in myth and symbol
is always for our salvation.

3

The Leafing Fig Tree

The First Sunday in Advent

Luke 21.29–33

Then he told them a parable: "Look at the fig tree and all the trees; as soon as they sprout leaves you can see for yourselves and know that summer is already near. So also, when you see these things taking place, you know that the kingdom of God is near. Truly I tell you, this generation will not pass away until all things have taken place. Heaven and earth will pass away, but my words will not pass away."

St. Andrew Lutheran Church
Andrews, North Carolina

The Leafing Fig Tree

The greening grass,
the leafing trees,
the budding flowers,
all announce the spring time.
Before the spring arrives,
the barren trees,
the biting cold,
the frozen turf
tell us that winter is here.

The seasons come and go,
each in its turn.
The signs that mark their coming,
The signs that mark their ending,
are visible
to the naked eye.
Even so there is mystery to it all.
A mystery
we cannot fathom,
though seed time and harvest,
winter cold and summer heat
follow upon each other
with constant regularity.

Advent

Advent
announces a new season for us:
a season of preparation,
a season portending
a great event in the near future.
Our calendar
is set for Day One today.
We enter a new season.
We enter a new Church Year.
How many there have been!

A thousand nine hundred years ago and more
our Scripture was penned

Bread? or Crumbs?

by a man named Luke.
He announced an Advent,
the coming of the Son of man.
His coming
would be with power and great glory.
His coming would mark the end of all seasons,
the end of the age.

He wrote,
"There will be signs in sun, moon, and stars.
Upon the earth distress among nations
in perplexity
at the roaring of the sea and the waves.
Men fainting with fear
and with foreboding
of what is coming on the world.
The powers of the heavens will be shaken."

He anticipated
the end would be very soon.
He warned
against dissipation and drunkenness,
about the cares of this life.
He said,
"That day will come suddenly like a snare.
It will come unexpectedly
upon all earth dwellers."
He challenged his audience,
"Watch, pray
that you may have strength to escape
the coming dreadful catastrophe.
Watch, pray
that you may be able to stand
before the Son of man."

Today begins Advent,
a new year in our church calendar.
Luke did not anticipate
there would be so many.
He was certain only a few years

remained on earth's calendar.
He wrote,
"This generation will not pass away
till all has taken place."
Many generations have come and gone
since he wrote these words.
How many times has there been distress
among nations?
How many time have the heavens
been shaken?
Great explosions marking
the birth of new stars,
perhaps new galaxies.
The roaring of the seas,
the raging of its billows,
the thunder of volcanoes.
All these have shaken the earth repeatedly.

The end is not yet!
Luke could not foresee
nineteen centuries and more!
He did not expect his century to run its course.
What is our expectation today?
Do we have Luke's perspective?
Or do we hold a modern view of this world?
Is it possible
the earth could come to an end suddenly
even in our generation?
Do we live as though today may be our last?
Or do we expect this world,
this universe,
to continue forever?

Everything about us says
we are not Lukan.
We are tooling up for many, many centuries
of life on earth.
Century twenty-one is upon us.
We foresee great and serious problems
to our existence:

Bread? or Crumbs?

over population,
over pollution,
a shortage of resources.
Life may end on planet Earth.
Earth may return to the barrenness
it knew eons ago.
Will the earth continue
another four and a half billions of years?
Will life, human life, survive?
Or will man disappear from the face of the earth?

What is the meaning,
the relevance of our lesson?
Are we moved to faith,
or to skepticism,
by the announcement that this world,
this age, is coming to a close?
Does the call of Luke rouse us
to watchfulness, to prayer?
Or do we simply yawn
and return to whatever is at hand?
Have we settled in for a long, comfortable,
extended life on earth?

Advent is a time for preparation,
a time for renewal,
a time for reappraisal,
a time to watch and pray.
Advent is fraught with meaning,
even though Luke's perspective
may not be our own.

Consider the Fig Tree

The leafing fig tree
announces that summer is near.
Our Advent time proclaims
the nearness of our celebration
of the birth of the Christ, our Savior.
He came,

The Leafing Fig Tree

born a child,
this one destined to be Savior and Lord.

At the time of his coming,
power was shrouded in weakness;
glory hidden in a mantle of flesh and blood.
The ones who looked upon that infant
could not foresee,
nor anticipate,
who he would become.
So it is with the leafing fig tree.
We know that summer is near,
but we do not know what summer will bring.
The future is not ours.
We cannot know it as we remember yesterday.
The future is ever before us,
hidden from our view.
We cannot determine it, or control it.
We can only live in it
as God gives us our days and years.

Advent announces the coming one.
Soon we celebrate
his coming in the flesh,
a coming
more than a thousand nine hundred years ago.
We look back to an event
that happened centuries ago.

We cannot look upon the face of that child,
just as we cannot look back upon
the face of those
who belong to the yester years.
Yet we celebrate his birth,
a birth vital and meaningful to us,
because we have sensed and felt the power
of this man, Jesus,
in our todays.

Bread? or Crumbs?

He lived!
He died!
His life, his death were not the life or death
of any other human.
His birth, his life,
his death have uniquely challenged
and powerfully changed the life, the death
and the destiny of everyone of us.
He lived! He spoke!
He acted in ways
that have become the model for us.
And more than our model,
for he opened doors to us;
doors that we could not have entered
if he had not lived, died, and lives again.

The leafing fig tree
announces that summer is near.
Summer,
the time for fruit bearing,
for sharing in all the bounty of the good earth.
Advent is that leafing fig tree.
Advent announces the nearness
of the One who came,
the One who comes,
the One who is here.

As God bountifully feeds and nourishes us
from the fruits of the good earth,
so God is here
to bountifully feed and nourish
from the fruits of the leafing fig tree.
Advent is the message
of the one who comes from God
to deliver us from the winter season,
from darkness and despair,
from hopelessness and non-fruit bearing.

Once more
we hear the glorious announcement.

The Leafing Fig Tree

Once more
we thrill to the message of hope:
the Christ child is born!
He has come.
God has not left us in darkness.
God has not left us
to suffer the just reward for our sinning
against him, against humanity,
against the good earth
he has so graciously given.

We celebrate
the birth of the Christ child,
not because it happened centuries ago,
but because of what is happening today
in our lives, in our world
because the Christ child
was given to us as the gift from God.
He is the leafing fig tree
bearing fruit,
nourishing us upon the life of God forever.
Through his birth, his life, his death,
and his living again,
we are brought near
to the God of our salvation,
who saves us from all that destroys
and brings our wonderful potential to naught.

We have been set free from bondage
to our ego, to the world,
to the powers of sin and evil,
from futility and meaninglessness,
from death,
to become the people of God in this world.
We are called to a new life
of righteousness,
of goodness, of nobility;
a people dedicated to truth and love
for every human on earth
and to the wonderful planet Earth

God has so graciously given
as the cocoon, the nest, for our good life.

We are free
to live as God's people in this world;
free to serve righteousness,
the good, the noble, the true.
We are the fruit of the leafing fig tree
through the redeeming power of his death,
through the life-giving power of his life.
We are a new people.
No more can we live to and for ourselves.
No more can we seek our own in everything we do.
Our lives our marvelously transformed
into the image and likeness
of that leafing fig tree
that God planted among us so long ago.

The Fruit Bearing Tree

We are the fruit of that planting:
we who believe God;
we who walk in his way;
we who tell the good news in work and word,
in song and by pen,
in lives devoted
to the will of our Creator,
our Redeemer and Lord.
The leafing fig tree
announces that summer is near.
Even now there is a great season of tomorrows
before us.
We tremble not,
we do not fear,
even though the earth be shaken,
even though the mountains fall into the sea.

God, our God, is here!
Here to take us in his loving arms,
to allay our fears, our anxieties.

The Leafing Fig Tree

Here to create within us faith and confidence
that our future is certain and assured.
The end of this world,
the end of our life on earth
cannot create fear and trembling,
hopelessness and despair.

The end of this world,
the end of our life,
means that God brings forth
a new heaven and a new earth fashioned
in righteousness and goodness forever!
The leafing fig tree
marks both the passing of the past
and the beginning of our future:
the end of lifelessness,
of hopelessness and futility,
the end of being and the beginning
of hope and joy,
of life without ending.

The leafing fig tree is
both the end of the old
and the beginning of a glorious future.
Now is the time for life,
strength, vigor, growth.
Life for us is no longer standing still
as we mark with sadness
the end of each day.
We lean forward into the future,
into our tomorrows;
tomorrows that will be better
than any yesterdays have been.
Luke was not mourning the past.
He was announcing a glorious, brilliant future.
The end of this age is not the end;
it is the beginning of that
which could not be
until the leafing of the fig tree.

Bread? or Crumbs?

The leafing tree marks the end!
The end to all
that bars the forward step,
the upward look,
the unending growth.
The kingdom of God
comes to glorious fulfillment!
The prospect is so wondrous, so glorious,
we can only await its coming with bated breath,
with eager longing,
with joyous expectation.

We do not await in idleness
with folded hands,
rocking away time in our easy chair day after day.
We are the leafing fig tree in our age;
copies of that leafing fig tree
that God planted long ago,
that leafing fig tree we recognize to be
the man Jesus.
As he comes alive in us,
we put forth roots and branches,
leaves and fruit.
Branches, leaves and fruit pleasing to God,
a blessing to all our brothers and sisters on earth.

God has given us
the signs of the times that are coming upon us.
They are the marks,
the fruits of our lives
indelibly imprinted upon others;
lives that radiate joy, peace, integrity,
faith and love.
We live on
in the lives of those who come after,
touched by our faithfulness
to the God of our creation,
of our redemption, and of our future.

The Leafing Fig Tree

"Do not let the world
squeeze you into its mold,"
says the Apostle.
The fruits of the leafing fig trees
of this world can only be sorrow,
strife, prejudice, hatred,
malice, selfishness,
pride and greed, to mention a few.

The fruit of God's leafing fig tree are
the gifts of the Spirit
manifested in our daily lives—
love, joy, peace,
generosity, kindness,
integrity, faithfulness, humility.
The future of God comes alive in
and through the leafing fig tree
that we become
when the Christ of this Season is born in us today.

When we are the leafing fig trees of God,
life in our homes,
in our community,
in our work place,
in our world of governance,
in the entire world of humanity is born anew
to a future that is bright and glorious
for all people and for all the earth.

The future is not some nebulous tomorrow!
The future is NOW!
What other future can there be
when we are God's leafing trees today?
God has given us this moment,
this day, this year
to be his leafing fig tree and to bear fruit for him.
Let us respond to the God of love,
the God of peace,
the God of the past,
of the present and of the future.

Bread? or Crumbs?

"Come!"
says our God,
"Be my leafing fig tree.
Come! Live! Grow!
Bear fruit for me!"

4

The Axe, the Tree, and the Fire

The Second Sunday in Advent

Matthew 3.1–12

In those days John the Baptist appeared in the wilderness of Judea, proclaiming, "Repent, for the kingdom of heaven has come near." This is the one of whom Isaiah the prophet spoke when he said,
"The voice of one crying out in the wilderness:
  'Prepare the way of the Lord,
  make his paths straight.'"
Now John wore clothing of camel's hair with a leather belt around his waist, and his food was locusts and wild honey. Then the people of Jerusalem and all Judea were going out to him, and all the region along the Jordan, and they were baptized by him in the river Jordan, confessing their sins. But when he saw many Pharisees and Sadducees coming for baptism, he said to them, "You brood of vipers! Who warned you to flee from the wrath to come? Bear fruit worthy of repentance. Do not presume to say to yourselves, 'We have Abraham as our ancestor;' for I tell you, God is able from these stones to raise up children to Abraham. Even now the axe is lying at the root of the trees; every tree therefore that does not bear good fruit is cut down and thrown into the fire.
"I baptize you with water for repentance, but one who is more powerful than I is coming after me; I am not worthy to carry his sandals. He will baptize you with the Holy Spirit and fire. His winnowing fork is in his hand, and he will clear his threshing floor and will gather his wheat into the granary; but the chaff he will burn with unquenchable fire."

Luther Memorial Church
Burbank, California

The Axe, the Tree, and the Fire

The axe,
honed to a fine edge
to hew down the tree
planted by God.
A tree that grew from a small seed.
A seed that germinated,
pushing its way through the earth,
growing to a great size,
to the time of fruit bearing.

The burning fire
consuming the tree
when lit by the torch.
The axe,
the tree,
the fire.
Symbols of a lesson from God.
Trees
are for fruit bearing.
The unfruitful tree is cut down,
cast into the fire
and burned.

The tree is a symbol in the lesson
of human beings,
of you and me.
The tree is also a symbol of
the community of God's people.
The axe and the fire:
Symbols of God's judgment
upon the persons or community
that do not heed the word of God
and bear fruit.

We are fashioned in God's image
to live gentle, kind,
loving lives,
showing the face of God
in all relationships of life.

The Messenger

There was a man sent from God.
John was his name.
He came preaching
in the wilderness of Judea.
What a strange arena for preaching.
Preaching is for people.

Can the message of God ever be
for bushes,
or cacti, or weeds and flowers?
For the plants that grow in the wilderness?

John the baptizer came
proclaiming the word of God
to a people
who had departed from the ways of God.
To a people
devoted to their own interests,
not to the concerns of God.
To a people
mouthing the name of God,
but worshipping no God other than the god of self.

John the baptizer came
preaching in the wilderness.
His message was heard,
the sound of his voice went forth
to all the inhabited regions.
His message
was carried on currents of wind
to the ears of many
in city and hamlet and to the countryside.

People came from far and near
to hear
this strange messenger from God
dressed
in a rough robe of camel's hair

with a leather strap for a belt.
A man
who ate the food of the wilderness,
locusts
and wild honey.

The messenger was serious.
His message severe,
"Repent!
The kingdom of heaven is at hand.
You brood of vipers!
who warned you to flee from the coming wrath?"
The heat
kindled by the fierce words
of this messenger of God
created great anxiety
in the bosoms of those who heard.

The fierce anger of God,
unleashed
by the burning words of the prophet,
roused the hearers to seek
a way of escape.
They came against their will,
drawn by the overpowering magnet of God.
Reason
advised them to flee,
to seek a safe haven,
to shut out
the burning words of the messenger of God.
They were drawn nevertheless
by a mysterious power
they could not resist.

How we play at religion.
How we tinker with the message from God,
comforting ourselves,
soothing our fears,
taking refuge in good deeds and respectability,
offering to God

Bread? or Crumbs?

substitutes and imitations
rather than the fruits
God expects from his planting.

No more!
The messenger of God,
not intimidated by the credentials
of the ones who came
so confidently:
Pharisees,
righteous Pharisees,
claiming to do more than God required.
Sadducees,
priestly Sadducees,
presiding over the rituals and sacrifices
that guaranteed
man's worthiness before God.

God's messenger,
terrible in zeal,
awesome in authority,
unbending in his stern proclamation:
God comes
looking for fruit from his people;
The fruits of kindness,
goodness, integrity,
humility, and faithfulness.

God is not a weak God,
a God we can satisfy
with a small basket of fruit.
God is the mighty Lord of heaven and earth.
God looks for
a total commitment
of heart and life from his people.

How can we,
earthly and sinful,
bargain with God?
Can we wheedle concessions from him

by our empty promises?
Can we whittle down his expectations?
"No!"
proclaims the messenger.
"Who warned you to flee from the coming wrath?
Even now the axe
is laid at the root of the tree.
Every tree
that does not bear fruit
is hewn down
and thrown into the fire and burned."

Is God like that?
Is the image of God
portrayed by the messenger
the image of God
we wear upon our hearts?
Is our God as stern as the messenger proclaims?
Is he not more lenient,
bowing to the wishes, the demands
of his people?
Is not God the God of love
who always manifests love and mercy?
Is God ever the axe wielder,
who hews down his own planting?
casting his tree into the fire to be burned?

Is the image of God
proclaimed by John a true image?
Or has John distorted the reality of our God?
Has John patterned
his image of God
after the image of man?
Humans vent their bitterness,
their frustrations and anger
at those they despise or hate?
Is God ever like that?

The Other Face of God

There is the loving face of God,
shining in the face of Jesus,
the face we see and know in the gospel.
God is rich in love and mercy.
God is the redeeming God,
the forgiving God;
the God who pleads with his people to come
to his banquet.

This is the face of God we cherish.
Our hope for the future
is grounded in the anticipation that God
is like our grandfather,
indulgent,
overlooking our faults and sins.
A God who reproves us for our sinning,
but not too severely.
A God who forgives no matter
how gross the wrong.

There is another face to God.
The face portrayed by this fierce preacher
of righteousness.
The God whose anger is roused by our sinning,
our indifference and waywardness,
our perverseness
in compromising truth and goodness
for personal gain.

God is not the indulgent grandfather.
God is our father,
a father who teaches us to live righteously,
to uphold truth and justice,
to practice daily
the ideals and values he has shared with us
through his son Jesus.
His intent is that all people everywhere
know the God of truth and love
through our example.

Advent celebrates
the coming of God to us.
God comes to right the wrongs in our lives.
He comes to discipline,
to correct, to purge from us
all that is sinful and false.
He comes to convert our selfishness
into generosity.
God is not a beggar with a cup
asking for small favors of us.

Advent
reveals the other face of God.
His intolerance of smallness,
of pettiness and meanness.
His displeasure with those petty sins
that discolor our deeds and words;
deeds and words
that fracture and fragment
the community of God's people
into self-interest groups.

The stern words of this preacher
of righteousness
are as necessary today as in days of old.
"Repent!
Bear fruit worthy of God.
Even now the axe of God will hew down
the unfruitful tree.
Even now the fire is ignited
to consume the tree not bearing fruit."

Fruit Bearers

God creates with purpose.
His works are never meaningless.
God did not shape and mold us
out of rude clay
to demonstrate his ingenuity.

Bread? or Crumbs?

God shaped and molded us
in his image
that we might be his face in the world:
loving, caring, generous,
sharing what we have received so bountifully
even as he has shared so bountifully with us.

It is the nature of a tree to bear fruit,
each tree according to its kind.
A tree that does not bear fruit
is contrary to nature.
A non-bearing tree is not worthy to exist.
The unfruitful tree must be hewn down,
uprooted,
thrown into the fire.
Such a tree does not fulfill the life purpose
implanted in it by God.

The lesson
of the axe, the tree, and the fire is:
we are God's trees
planted upon the good earth
to bear fruit
according to the nature within us.
We are created
in the image of God
that we might show the face of God
to one another
and to the world.

The face of God
unveiled
in the face of Jesus is to be the face
we show to the world:
the face of love,
the compassionate face,
the joyful face,
the gentle, kindly face
shown even to the wayward and fallen.

But also the stern face,
unyielding against bigotry,
hypocrisy and pretense;
against all smallness of mind and spirit.
The nature in us planted by God is
to bear the fruits of the Spirit—
love, joy, peace and goodwill,
kindness and gentleness,
truthfulness and integrity,
generosity,
and a forgiving spirit.

We are the trees of God,
his pleasant planting.
Our life's role and purpose is
to bear the fruit of God
in our thoughts, our words and deeds.
Even now we are being measured
by the yardstick of God
according to the fruits we bear
or do not bear
in our daily life.

The unfruitful tree,
the tree that does not show the face of God
to the world
and to one another
will be hewn down by the axe of God
and cast into the God's unquenchable fire.

God's message to us at Advent
is a message of love,
but also a stern and forbidding message
to all who do not take God seriously.
A message vital for us
to hear.
A message calling us to account
before God
for our stewardship of all
he has entrusted to us.

Bread? or Crumbs?

Do we bring forth the good fruits of the Spirit
in the daily relationships of life?
Or are we unfruitful trees
in God's forest of trees on earth?

The axe,
the tree,
the fire!
The focus of Advent!
God comes in judgment to prune
and cleanse us from all wickedness,
malice and anger,
pride and self-righteousness,
pretense and hypocrisy,
bigotry and prejudice,
carelessness and indifference,
greed and covetousness,
lust and bitterness.

Advent is God's time
to transform us from unfruitful trees
into fruit bearing trees
ever showing the face of God
to the world and to one another.
The axe, the tree, the fire
are powerful symbols
calling us to account before God today.

5

Light and Darkness

The Third Sunday in Advent

John 1.6–8

There was a man sent from God, whose name was John. He came as a witness to testify to the light, so that all might believe through him. He himself was not the light, but he came to testify to the light. The true light, which enlightens everyone, was coming into the world.

Luther Memorial Church
Burbank, California

Light and Darkness

Light
and darkness!
The contrasting conditions
for our daily existence.
We walk securely
in the light of day
without fear of stumbling and falling.
We walk warily
in the darkness of the night,
often in fear and anxiety,
even foreboding.

Light is associated
with truth and right,
with goodness and honesty.
Darkness is associated
with falsehood and wrong,
with evil and dishonesty.

Light and darkness
are symbolic.
The terms are used figuratively
in early Christian writings
to portray
spiritual truth.

"The day is far spent.
Night is at hand.
Let us cast off the works of darkness
and put on
the garments of light,"
said the Apostle.

The setting for our story
of the birth of the Christ child
is the darkness of night.
There was no room in the inn
the night

Bread? or Crumbs?

Joseph and Mary
sought lodging in Bethlehem.

There were shepherds in the field
that night
keeping watch over their flocks.
Night and darkness
are the settings
for the coming of the light of the world
into our midst.

The prophet,
near eight centuries before
the birth of the Savior,
told of the coming
of salvation from God in these words,
"The people
who walked in darkness
have seen a great light;
those who dwelt in a land of deep darkness,
on them has light shined."

There was a long range anticipation
that the darkness
of sin and evil
would be turned back
and overthrown.
The glory of the Lord would shine,
lighting the pathways
of truth and right,
revealing to humankind
a future of joy and peace.

The ultimate goal
is existence without darkness.
The writer of the Apocalypse announces
that at the end of earthly existence,
there will be a new heaven and a new earth.
a time and a place
"where there will be no night."

Light and Darkness

A Man from God

There was a man sent from God
whose name was John.
He came
to be a witness to the light
that all might believe through him.
He was not the light.
He came
as the forerunner of a new light,
a heavenly light,
that was even now breaking into the world.
He came
to testify to the light.

A man from God!
What kind of man is this?
How does this man differ from other men?
Not in size.
Not in appearance.
Not in human traits.

There was nothing about this man
that distinguished him
from men in general
except his life style.
He lived in a desert region.
His attire was not traditional,
nor was his diet.
He dressed in a robe of camel's hair,
a leather belt around his waist.
He ate locusts and wild honey.

These are only incidental,
not substantial,
differences.
God does not choose men or women
because of a certain life style,
or a particular dress or diet.

Bread? or Crumbs?

A man from God!
What does this tell us about John?
He was chosen,
appointed and anointed
to be a prophet,
a spokesman for God.

Was there something about his parentage?
his birth and early training
that distinguished him?
That led God to choose him
from all the men of that day
to be a witness
to the light?

Does God single out certain persons
to be spokesmen and spokeswomen?
To be his special witnesses,
because there is something godlike
that distinguishes them?

Did the mantle of God
fall upon John,
because there was something distinguished,
or unique about him
that set him apart from
every other man or woman of the day?

I was born
in the year of our Lord, 1917.
A year
when a great conflagration
was devastating Europe.
Thousands of men, women, and children
were sacrificed
upon the altar of the war god that year,
bloody victims
of our inhumanity and brutality to one another.

Light and Darkness

My elder brother
was born in the year of our Lord, 1914.
Another brother
in the year of our Lord, 1918.
A twin brother and sister
in the year of our Lord, 1924.

Born of the same parentage.
Reared in the same home environment.
Our religious training in the same church community,
Educated in the same school system.
I, alone of the five,
had this inner compulsion
to enter the ministry as my calling from God.

The elder brother
a tool and dye maker in a factory.
The next brother a university professor
in psychology.
The younger brother an electrical engineer.
The sister a nurse.

The calling is from God.
The response to the calling is ours to give.
The calling into ministry
is not greater
than the calling into any other vocation in life.
Luther said,
"The housewife who sweeps the kitchen floor
to the glory of God,
does as noble a service
as the pastor who preaches the sermon."

We are called to respond to our calling
with wholehearted devotion
serving faithfully, honestly,
in the vocation God has called us to service.
Our responses
to our calling may be very different.

Bread? or Crumbs?

Some responses may be half-hearted and insincere.
Some who are called by God
to ministry may say,
"Not today, Lord.
Someday, but not today."
Others may respond from ulterior motives.
A young man,
in his senior year at one of our seminaries
came to the guidance counselor
deeply troubled.

He confessed that he was entering the ministry
because in his childhood
his pastor had been in a terrible car accident.
It seemed impossible for anyone to survive.
Yet the pastor was unscathed.
As a young lad he reasoned,
"If God protects pastors thus,
I want to be a pastor."
He could not continue in that calling
as the light of truth dawned
in his consciousness.

I was visiting in the home of one of my parishioners.
The father, the son, and I
involved in conversation,
when the son said,
"I want to be a pastor when I grow up."
The father said,
"No, you don't want to be a pastor.
You know how they treat Pastor Swanson."
The son entered the field of business instead.

John
was a man sent from God.
The Spirit of God
drove him into the wilderness,
although he should have followed
in his father's footsteps,
a priest serving God in the temple.

Light and Darkness

At the appropriate time,
he heard the call of God,
"Go, proclaim my word of truth to my people.
Go, announce the Coming One,
the light of the world."

There were days and years of preparation,
of discipline,
before he made his debut
as the prophet,
the spokesman for God.

The calling from God
was so clear, so powerful,
that he accepted this mandate
without hesitation
or complaint.
A man from God!
Unique and special because he responded
with a great 'Amen!'
"Here am I, Lord. Send me."

A Witness to the Light

John
became a witness to the light.
Light and truth—
two facets to the face of God.
There is darkness in us;
the darkness of sin and wickedness,
of willfulness and self-centeredness.

Light alone
has the power to drive out darkness.
We cannot control,
or manage, our own willful nature.
Sin and wickedness
grow and multiply in us
without the truth and the light of God.

Bread? or Crumbs?

There are those who will not come
into the light,
even though they have been exposed to the light
in home and church.
Jesus said,
"Light has come into the world;
but many loved darkness rather than light,
because their works are evil."

What a sad commentary
upon a people
created in the image of God,
blessed with so many gifts and opportunities,
exposed to the wondrous light of God,
yet preferring darkness to light,
choosing
to live in the shadow,
shrouded from the light and truth of God.

A sadder truth is
that many choose to live in a gray belt.
Living neither in darkness
nor in the light.
Living in a half-way house.
Accepting enough of the light of God
as an insurance policy
to feel safe and secure,
but not enough to spoil a life style
devoted to pleasure,
wealth, or power.

How much of the light of God
is enough
to assure God's blessing in this life
and in the life to come?
How many live in a kind of hell on earth,
because they refuse to live
in heaven now!

Light and Darkness

John was driven by an inner compulsion,
by the Spirit of God,
to bear witness to the light.
Never could he be half-hearted
or lukewarm.
He was on fire for God.

He proclaimed
with all the strength and fervor of his being,
"I am a voice
crying out in the wilderness,
Make straight the way of the Lord."
He threw caution to the winds.
He forsook that tendency within all of us
to set our own interests
above the will of God.
He would not water down the message of God
so as not to offend his audience.

He was faithful even to death
as a witness to the light.
He proclaimed with fervor
that God is not pleased with darkness,
or even with shades of gray.
The eternal God calls to full commitment,
to eschew darkness,
to walk in the light,
to proclaim the truth of God
without fear and favor.

I look at the headlines
of the Los Angeles Times for December 11.
What catches my eye?
Former State Senator Paul Carpenter,
member of the State Board of Equalization,
sentenced to twelve years in prison
for extortion.

I read about nine Los Angeles police officers,
on special assignment

Bread? or Crumbs?

for drug enforcement,
found guilty
of stealing confiscated drugs and money
for their own use.

Who are these men?
Have they been exposed to the light?
To the truth of God?
Without question.
Some of them probably church members
from childhood.
They have walked in the light,
but they have chosen darkness rather than light.

I read the sad story
of an AIDS epidemic in Laguna Beach.
Of medical doctors hosting
three day orgies for their clients.
Of a beautiful young man
with exceptional physical attributes
who took his own life
when the pain became too great.
Who wrote for his memorial service
conducted in a church,
"I have had a ball.
I enjoyed every minute of it."

What sad commentaries of failures
and perversions
of the light from God our Creator.
As I reflect upon these stories of wasted lives,
I must ask the question,
"Have I contributed in any way
to such misunderstandings,
to such perversions,
of truth and right?
Have I failed to walk in the light of God?
To witness
to the light by my every deed and word and attitude?

Light and Darkness

Can it be
that my unwillingness
to be totally committed to the light,
to be satisfied with the gray,
has contributed
to the breakdown of the moral fiber
of a brother or a sister
who has looked to me as a role model?

When we live in the gray belt,
not in the light,
are we responsible
for the spiritual death of another?
Are we guilty of compromising truth,
integrity and honesty
justice and equality,
out of fear or self-interest?

What is the qualitative difference
between a Paul Carpenter,
or a police officer gone astray,
or an AIDS victim
who had a ball while it lasted,
and me,
in the sight of God?

Brothers and sisters in Christ.
We have an awesome responsibility
as witnesses to the light.
We are called and consecrated
to be honest and faithful to God,
to love our neighbor and our enemy,
to be a light in the world
by every manifestation of who we are
and by all we think and do and say.

How has our relationship to God
and our commitment to the truth of God
impacted the lives of those around us?
We are called to be models

Bread? or Crumbs?

of the Christ-like life in the world;
our lights shining brightly
to those who are in darkness.

As pastors we struggle perennially
with the question,
When is a church member
both a church member
and a believing, practicing Christian?

There are many on the church rolls who are so casual
about church attendance,
about Bible study and prayer,
about participation
and support of the mission of the church.
The attitude:
It isn't a big deal.
I will become serious one of these days.

It reminds me of one of the church members
of my home church in Minnesota,
who, on his deathbed,
promised God he would change his ways
if he had another chance.
He recovered,
only to revert to his old ways
of indifference and denial.

There is a commandment
given by God long ago to his people,
the basic commandment of all,
"You shall have no other gods."
Without this foundation for our faith and life,
we are only toying with the light.
We are in love with darkness rather than light.

It is probable
that the examples cited,
Paul Carpenter, police officers, an AIDS victim,
gradually slipped into darkness,

Light and Darkness

beginning with a small deed of shading truth.
Then from small beginnings,
the seed germinated and grew
into a life style of dishonesty and corruption.
The pattern accelerated
as the light of the truth of God waned,
sputtered, and went out.

Brothers and sisters in Christ,
we are at risk
whenever we do not walk in the light,
when we walk in a gray shadow,
or even in the darkness of night.

There was a man sent from God
to witness to the light,
so that all might believe through him.
Light and faith,
inseparable,
for without faith there cannot be light.

How many are adrift
in a morass of relative values and ideals,
subject to every pleasing wind
of doctrine
that is proclaimed so freely
by the hucksters of religion
in the name of Christ.
How many have exchanged the true light
for a shadowy gray,
because it is made so easy to be Christian
without the light giver
at the very heart of our being.

We are called to walk in the light.
To follow the light of the world,
the Christ
who gave his life
that we might die to self, to sin,
to our ego centeredness.

Bread? or Crumbs?

To die with Christ daily and to rise
from the waters of our baptism
to the life of faith
devoted to light and love and joy.

Hallelujah!
Christ, our Savior, is born.

6

Consider the Candle

The Fourth Sunday in Advent

Matthew 1.18–25

Now the birth of Jesus the Messiah took place in this way. When his mother Mary had been engaged to Joseph, but before they lived together, she was found to be with child from the Holy Spirit. Her husband Joseph, being a righteous man and unwilling to expose her to public disgrace, planned to dismiss her quietly. But just when he had resolved to do this, an angel of the Lord appeared to him in a dream and said, "Joseph, son of David, do not be afraid to take Mary as your wife, for the child conceived in her is of the Holy Spirit. She will bear a son, and you are to name him Jesus, for he will save his people from their sins." All this took place to fulfill what had been spoken through the prophet:
"Look, the virgin shall conceive
and bear a son,
and they shall name him Emmanuel,"
which means "God is with us." When Joseph awoke from sleep, he did as the angel of the Lord commanded him; he took her as his wife, but had no married relations with her until she had borne a son; and he named him Jesus.

St. Andrew Lutheran Church
Andrews, North Carolina

Consider the Candle

Consider the candle!
Candles in the chancel,
only a decoration to some worshippers.
To those who know and understand
their meaning and purpose,
the candle teaches a profound spiritual truth.
The candle,
a symbol of Jesus who said,
"I am the light of the world."

From ancient times
it was the custom of the church
to place two single candles
in the chancel
or upon the altar.
The candles symbolize
the two natures of Jesus the Christ,
the divine and the human.

This is meaningful today
as we pause to reflect upon the wonder
of God's love.
The incarnation,
the birth of our Lord Jesus Christ.

We believe
and we confess that
"Jesus is true God conceived
of the Holy Spirit
and that Jesus is true man
born of the virgin Mary."

The word,
the divine word of God,
became flesh and lived among us.
We cannot fully comprehend
or explain
the divine wonder, the mystery.

Bread? or Crumbs?

We can only bow humbly
in wonder and awe
before this marvel of God.

To the agnostic,
to the unbeliever,
it is an impossibility for God to become human.
So it is.
For the one without faith cannot know
what is possible for God.

If Mary had been an agnostic,
an unbeliever,
she would not have been chosen
by God
to be the mother of God.

Mary,
of all the young maidens of Israel,
chosen for this sacred and holy motherhood
because she had that quality of faith
that believed God.
She trusted
that nothing was impossible to the God of Israel.

Two candles on the altar
symbolize the two natures of the Christ.
Our sermon, however,
is not intended to be a lesson in liturgics.
Let us consider
the purpose and role of the candle in our lives.

A candle gives light
so that we might find our way
through the darkness of night.
To give light,
the candle must be consumed,
devoured by fire.

Consider the Candle

Our candle is wax.
It burns for a time,
it gives light.
It is soon gone, consumed by the flame.
In being consumed, the candle gives light
to all
in the range of its brilliance.

This is the lesson for today.
The life
dedicated to the service of God
and to humanity
is like the candle.

A Burning and a Shining Light

The life of John the Baptizer reminds us
of a candle.
Jesus said to the Jews,
"You sent to John.
He has borne witness to the truth.
He was a burning and shining lamp.
You were willing to rejoice for a while
in his light."

John was a burning and shining lamp.
His light shone for a season.
His life was consumed by giving light.
Let us recall
the marvelous nature of his birth.
His parents,
Zechariah and Elizabeth,
were advanced in years.

The father priest
was burning incense in the temple
at the hour of prayer.
An angel of God appeared.
Zechariah's prayer was answered.
God promised a son

though Elizabeth was beyond the age
for child bearing.
The promise of God was marvelously fulfilled.

We read in our gospel
that the child grew and became strong in spirit.
Born to be a priest,
he was in the wilderness
until the day
of his manifestation to Israel.

In the fifteenth year
of the reign of Tiberius Caesar,
the word of God
came to John in the wilderness,
and he went into all the region of the wilderness
preaching.

John's ministry was brief.
There is only a hint of chronology.
He preached for a few months or a year.
Then his life was snuffed out.

He was a herald
sent to announce the coming one.
He proclaimed God's word
to prepare
the hearts of all people
for the coming of the Messiah, the Savior.

When Jesus came preaching,
John's work was done.
In that brief span of a few months or a year,
John burned
and shone as a candle
to the glory of God.

He shone,
a bright light in a dark place.
He came to a world of people

Consider the Candle

without hope,
weary of sin and wickedness,
ignorant of their purpose in life
and of the will of God.
He came to announce God's way,
God's call to repentance,
to righteousness and holiness.

He announced,
All who come to God,
seeking salvation and life,
must come with clean hands and pure hearts.
The Spirit of God
inspired him to proclaim his message
with fervor and power.

He preached
with all fervor and zeal,
with all his energy.
He called on all to repent,
to turn from wickedness
to serve the living and true God.

His zeal was costly
from our point of view.
After a few months to a year,
his head was laid upon a chopping block.
He became the victim
of the ruler whose sin he condemned.

As the candle flames brightly
when lit by a torch,
as a candle shines in the darkness for a season
to give light,
so John, kindled by the Spirit of God,
became a blazing light
pointing to God's high and holy demand,
lighting the way
that we might know God's will for us.

Bread? or Crumbs?

As a candle burns itself out
in bringing light to us,
so John soon burned out
in the service of God.
In the brief span of his life,
John made a lasting impact upon all
who came within the hearing of his voice.

His light blazed brightly for a time.
Then that light was rudely extinguished.
We may ask,
Was it worthwhile?
Was it a life well spent?
Did John serve a good and useful purpose?
Was the value of his life
equal to the sacrifice he made?
Was his talent wasted?

Did he realize his full potential of body,
mind and spirit?
With all his energy and talent
John could have been a famous surgeon,
a lawyer, a merchant,
a teacher, a statesman,
a priest.

There are so many callings
of greater importance
than that of a prophet.
John could have lived a long, useful life
in another calling.
He might have earned honor and acclaim.

But in the prime of life,
when his talents and strength
were at their fullest,
John's life,
as a guttered candle,
was snuffed out,
and his disciples laid a headless corpse
in an unknown grave.

He was a burning and shining light!
His life was brief.
He did not burn and shine in vain!
The body of flesh was soon gone,
but the spirit of John lives on.

The light he kindled
did not go out.
No, not in two thousand years.
His light
still shines and radiates in our dark world
to the glory and majesty of God.

He pointed to Jesus, the coming one,
the light of the world.
The one who comes from God
as Savior of the world.
The one who overcomes all the powers of sin and death.

Jesus Christ
is the light of the world.
The one who cleanses from sin.
Through his gracious forgiveness
we enter the presence of God
with clean hands
and a pure heart.

Jesus Christ
is the light of the world.
He makes known the truth of God.
He brings us to our heavenly Father
in childhood
and sustains us throughout our life on earth.
He leads us in paths of righteousness.

We are freed from anxiety and fear
when we walk in his light.
Freed from the terror of the darkness of sin.
He is our light.

He brings heaven to earth.
We share in that blessedness even now.

John was a burning and shining light!
His life was not in vain.
He was the beacon
pointing to the light of the world.
He pointed to the one
who is the source
of our hope, our joy, our peace.

To Burn and to Shine

This is the lesson of the candle.
If we shine for Jesus
in this dark world,
we must burn.
A candle is consumed in order to shine.

If we want to reach the heights
in any profession or calling,
we must pay the cost to the last penny.
No sacrifice can be too great.
No obstacle too impossible.
No effort too tiring.
The road to glory is not an easy road.
The gate is narrow and the way difficult.
Success is attained
only through persistent, untiring effort.

In a higher sense,
the road to glory,
the road to the heights of heaven
is never an easy way.
Often we have this strange, false notion
that we can have Jesus
without cost.

In spite of the word of God
proclaimed by John

Consider the Candle

and by Jesus,
we act as though we can live as we please
without interference or guidance from above.
To be Christian,
To follow our Lord Jesus Christ,
we must be his candle,
lighted to burn and to shine for him.

A candle is useless until it is lighted,
kindled into flame.
Lighted,
the candle is consumed.
It gives light.
Only then does the candle
fulfill the purpose for which it is created.

So it is!
We too are useless in the community
of God's people
until we are willing to burn and to shine.
Brothers and sisters in Christ!
How can we be complacent,
or self-satisfied?
How can we be careless and indifferent
about godliness?
How can we be unconcerned or disinterested
in our neighbor's plight?
Not when we are lighted as a candle
by Jesus Christ our Lord.

We are God's candles,
kindled into flame
by the light of the world.
Now we reflect his radiance and glory
in the world around us.
The cost is high
to be the light God would have us be.
See how quickly
John was consumed burning and shining for him.
See how our Lord Jesus

was consumed by the cruel cross
to become the light of the world.

He too was consumed as a candle
that his light might shine
into the farthest reaches of the earth,
to bring salvation
and the life in God to all people.

If we do not shine for him.
If we are not lights in the world
beckoning, inviting to Christ,
is it that we fear
to burn for him?

Do we fear
being consumed by this one passion?
Are we shamed
to become nobody
to be somebody for the Christ?
How difficult a decision
to become a candle!
To lay aside ambition and self-desire,
to be willing to burn
and shine for him!

This is why we were baptized into Christ.
This is our motivation to be Christian in this world.
This is how we fulfill
God's intent
when he created us out of the dust of the earth.

Behold the candle!
How brightly it shines!
What promise and hope in its light
to a world trapped in darkness.
Christ Jesus is the light of the world
in and through us.

Consider the Candle

Will you be his candle?
Are you kindled by the Spirit of God
to burn and shine for him?
Here rests our hope for heaven on earth.
God has entrusted to us
some one out there
who walks in darkness,
stumbling through life,
yearning, longing to become a flame
for the light of the world.

The destiny of that one
and of many another
rests with us
to fulfill our calling to be candles
burning and shining for him.

Will you be his candle?
Will you burn and shine for him?
Spreading the radiance
of his glory,
of his peace and joy
wherever you are?

This is God's call
to you and to me
Today.

7

No Room in the Inn

Christmas Eve, 1983

Luke 2.1–7

In those days a decree went out from Emperor Augustus that all the world should be registered. This was the first registration and was taken while Quirinius was governor of Syria. All went to their own towns to be registered. Joseph also went from the town of Nazareth in Galilee to Judea, to the city of David called Bethlehem, because he was descended from the house and family of David. He went to be registered with Mary, to whom he was engaged and who was expecting a child. While they were there the time came for her to deliver her child. And she gave birth to her firstborn son and wrapped him in bands of cloth, and laid him in a manger, because there was no place for them in the inn.

Angelica Lutheran Church
Los Angeles, California

No Room in the Inn

The weary traveler
at the close of day,
seeks refuge for the night.
He knocks
at the innkeeper's door.
"Sorry,"
said the innkeeper.
"No room in the inn this night."

We have known the frustration,
the discouragement,
when seeking lodging without a reservation.
How often have we heard the solemn word,
"Sorry,
No room in the inn this night."

What to do?
Drive on?
Seek elsewhere?
Sleep in the car? or under the stars?
We too have made our improvisations,
because we did not have
the magic reservation.

No Room in Bethlehem

Long ago
and far away
a young couple traveled over the hills
of Judea
to Bethlehem.
Did they walk
Or did they ride?
Probably they trudged the dusty road.
with a staff
for a support.
They were simple people of modest means.

Bread? or Crumbs?

When the long day ended,
They came to an inn in the village of Bethlehem.
The inn was crowded.
They heard the innkeeper gruffly say,
"Sorry,
No room in the inn this night."
"My wife is exhausted from our journey,"
said the traveler.
"Sorry,
Did you have a reservation?"
"No,"
said the traveler,
"My wife is heavy with child.
We need a room out of the cold
to spend the night."
"Sorry,"
Replied the innkeeper,
"I have no room.
But there is a stable
in the rear.
Why don't you spend the night there?"

So they made preparations for the night
with straw for a bed.
They ate simply.
A crust of dried bread.
A few dried figs.
A cup of water.
Then in the night it happened.
The birth pangs began.
No doctor.
No nurse in attendance.
The young husband serving as midwife.

The anxiety,
The fear
that gripped his heart!
How to know what to do?
A new experience for this young father to be.
The moans of pain.

No Room in the Inn

The terrible pressure.
The cry of the new born child.
The relief, the joy
that a child was born into the world.

Here they were
far from home.
Unprepared for this birth.
They used what cloths they had
to wrap the little child.
Children have been born in strange places
and under unusual circumstances.
Many children are born in similar,
if not poorer circumstances today.

Who cares?
Not the innkeeper.
Not the travelers cozy by the fireside
on a brisk winter evening.
Not the townspeople taking their rest.
Oblivious that a child is born.
So many children are born this night
without even a father to assist
their entry into the world.

Do we care?
Are we even aware?
If Joseph and Mary had come to an inn
in our town,
only to find there was no room,
would we have offered shelter?

Would we have taken them in,
these strangers?
Hardly!
It would be inconvenient,
or we would have great fear.
There are so many bad things that happen
when we show hospitality
to strangers.

Bread? or Crumbs?

Yet our scripture directs us,
"Show hospitality to strangers."
How are we to know
whether the strangers are trustworthy?
Or clean?
Whether they can return the favor
in the future?
Not all travelers who come to the door
are Josephs and Marys.
There are so many considerations
outweighing
the command of love
to show hospitality to strangers.

"What a Bad innkeeper,"
we say.
It is his business to provide room
for travelers.
Should not he be concerned for people
with special needs?
A young wife about to give birth?
A young couple without a roof
over their heads?
The problem is his, not mine.
I have a right to privacy.
I am not in the public housing business.

Or, let the traveler beware.
Let him make preparations in advance.
Let him plan so that he does not create
his own problem,
so the innkeeper does not need to say,
"No room in the inn."

The Innkeeper

The birth of a child
in a stable
is not a significant event.
Who noticed the birth of this child

No Room in the Inn

that night in Bethlehem.
Not the innkeeper.
Not the travelers safely housed in the inn.
Only a few shepherds with a strange tale
of a great light,
of an angel,
of a heavenly chorus singing,
"Glory to God in the highest."

Children born in stables
are not very important people.
They cannot be,
or they would be born in more suitable places,
a home or a hospital.
Nevertheless, forth from a stable at Bethlehem
came one destined by God
to be our Savior.
He is an important person to us.
That is why we are here.

Is it enough that we come to worship?
To light our candle
in the darkness of this night?
Is it enough that we sing our carols,
our songs of joy?
Is it enough that we greet one another
in a friendly way?
Wishing each other a merry Christmas?
Is it enough that we send a greeting,
or a gift
to the one who will do the same in return?
Is it enough that we gather in our homes
with our dear ones
to celebrate this event?
Are there not people out there
knocking at the door,
seeking refuge for the night?
Who hear the dismal voice of the innkeeper,
"Sorry,
No room in the inn?"

Bread? or Crumbs?

The innkeeper was no rascal,
no scoundrel was he.
He was a good Bethlehem Jew,
anxious to serve,
to have a good business relation with his clients.

He did the best he could that night.
There was no room in the inn.
He opened his stable to the young couple.
Even his stable could have been closed to them,
if he had wanted it so.
He was not a heartless man.
Perhaps he could have done more.
Thoughtless, perhaps!
Heartless, No!

The innkeeper is the role
we play this night.
We are the innkeepers of the world.
We have so much from God—
house and home,
family and dear ones,
food and drink,
money and goods,
peace and health.
And more!
We have the most wonderful gift of God's love—
the gift of his son,
our Savior and Lord.

What are innkeepers to do
when strangers,
or when the Christ comes to our door?
Should we say,
"Sorry,
No room in the inn?
I have a stable back there."

No Room in the Inn

Is that where we house the Christ who comes?
the Christ who is here with us
this night?
Do we have a little place out in the back?
A shed, a garage,
or even a little doghouse for him?

Yes!
This is often the sum total
of our hospitality.
We worship the glitter and the glow.
We keep the traditions alive.
We sing and make merry.
We eat our roast turkey
even while travelers are
knocking at our door.

What do we say to them?
"Sorry,
No room in the inn?"
There are homeless people out there,
naked, starving.
People seeking a home,
driven from their land
with nothing but themselves to offer.

There are homeless people on our doorstep,
living in tents and vans,
camping in parks,
even in alleys and doorways.
Forbidden even these poor accommodations
by the lords of the earth.

The concern of the innkeeper
that night
was for his guests housed in his inn.
He did what he could for those
who came without a reservation.

What of those who knock at our door?
Who have no reservations with us?
Do we owe them anything?
Are they our kind of people?
Is it not enough that we care for our own?
Do we say to them
"Sorry,
No room in the inn?"

Room in the Inn

The one who was born
in the stable that night at Bethlehem
turned out to be
a great one
Our place of birth,
our origins,
Do not determine the kind of person
we may be.

God is the Lord of history.
He chooses from among us
the simple,
the humble.
The ones from among us
who will carry forward his will in the world.

He looks for commitment,
for integrity,
compassion,
and a concern for people.
He looks for those who will gladly say,
"Yes,
There is room in the inn tonight."

Jesus
was one of us,
a man of flesh and blood.
He matches the description of a man
described by the prophet long ago.

No Room in the Inn

"He had no form nor attractiveness
that we should look up to him.
He had no beauty
that we should desire him."

There was nothing about these travelers,
knocking
at the innkeepers door
that impelled him to give up
his own room for them.

There is nothing that impels us,
God's innkeepers of the world
to open our hearts,
to open our homes to the stranger,
to the homeless,
to the naked,
to the hungry people
who come knocking at our door.
What can turn us from our preoccupation
with our celebration,
with our business at hand,
from whatever is important to us,
to become God's innkeepers
in our world today?

Innkeepers of the world!
We will only do what God wants us to do
when the Christ
we celebrate this night
has taken up lodging in our hearts
and in our lives.

Only when the Christ has a firm grip upon us,
only when he squeezes the selfishness
out of us;
the selfishness that rules our lives,
that prevents us from opening our doors
to the stranger,
to the hungry,

to the spiritually sick,
knocking,
pleading
for a room for the night.

Yes!
We, God's innkeepers, have the word
that frees us
from deadly selfishness.
God addresses us with that very word now.
"There is born to you
a Savior,
who is Christ the Lord."

This word of God, and only this word,
will unlock the gates,
open the doors,
flood our hearts with compassion and love
for people in need.
Especially in need for God in their lives.
This word of God alone
turns us inside out,
so that our concern, our care,
our love is
for the traveler without a room for the night.

Never again can we say,
"Sorry,
No room in the inn?"
When the Christ comes,
when he penetrates to the very depth of our being,
when he abides with us,
there is room.
Room
for the traveler
who seeks a place among God's people.

There is room in our hearts,
in our homes,
in our fellowship,

No Room in the Inn

in our church.
There is room.
Yes, there is room
when the Christ is the center of our life.

8

The Weeping Rachel

The Sunday after Christmas

Matthew 2.13–18

Now after they had left, an angel of the Lord appeared to Joseph in a dream and said, "Get up, take the child and his mother, and flee to Egypt, and remain there until I tell you; for Herod is about to search for the child, to destroy him." Then Joseph got up, took the child and his mother by night, and went to Egypt, and remained there until the death of Herod. This was to fulfill what had been spoken by the Lord through the prophet, "Out of Egypt I have called my son."

When Herod saw that he had been tricked by the wise men, he was infuriated, and he sent and killed all the children in and around Bethlehem who were two years old or under, according to the time he had learned from the wise men. Then was fulfilled what had been spoken through the prophet Jeremiah,

"A voice was heard in Ramah,
wailing and loud lamentation,
Rachel weeping for her children;
she refused to be consoled,
because they were no more."

Luther Memorial Church
Burbank, California

The Weeping Rachel

Rachel!
Wife of the patriarch Jacob.
Mother of Joseph and Benjamin,
fathers of three of the twelve tribes of Israel.
Jacob's second wife,
but his first love.

Jacob!
The supplanter
who stole his brother Esau's birthright
and blessing by deceit.
When Esau threatened to kill him,
Jacob fled to Haran in Mesopotamia.
There he met Rachel,
daughter of Laban.

It was love at first sight.
Rachel was lovely and beautiful.
Jacob said
to his uncle Laban,
"I will work seven years for you
for the hand of Rachel
to be my wife."

When the seven years were completed,
Laban deceived Jacob.
He gave his eldest daughter, Leah,
to Jacob to be his wife.
The deceiver became the deceived.
One of the most poignant sentences in the Old Testament
describe that wedding,
"In the morning it was Leah."

The Story

Jacob loved Rachel.
He worked another seven years to gain her
for his bride.
Years passed.

Bread? or Crumbs?

Laban and Jacob were rivals,
each seeking to outdo the other
by deceit and treachery.
Jacob's union with Leah was fruitful.
Six sons and two sons
by her handmaid.
Only one son born to Rachel,
Joseph,
whom his father favored.

There was a deep ache in the heart of Jacob
to return home to Canaan.
There were two problems:
How to escape from Laban?
How to avoid death at the hand of brother Esau
who had sworn to kill him?

Jacob departed from Haran
by stealth under the cover of darkness.
Laban was far from home in his fields.
On the way
there was a strange encounter
with a mysterious stranger
on the banks of the river Jabbak.
Jacob learned,
as he wrestled all night,
that God's promise
was a gift bestowed,
never to be snatched by strength or duplicity.
Jacob receive a new name that night,
Israel,
"He who strives with God."

His meeting with Esau was amicable.
Esau forgave brother Jacob.
There was great sorrow also
as they journeyed to Canaan,
the land of promise.
Rachel,
Jacob's beloved

died giving birth to her second son.
She named her child,
Benoni,
meaning "Son of sorrow,"
but Jacob called him Benjamin.

There was weeping and wailing
as Jacob buried
his beloved on the way to Bethlehem.

The Word of the Prophet

Time passed.
History unfolded
like a giant panorama across the pages of time.
Jacob and his sons
took refuge in Egypt in a time of famine.
Joseph,
son of Rachel,
sold into slavery by his wicked brothers
became their savior.

When Jacob and Joseph were no more,
there arose a Pharaoh who knew not Joseph.
A Pharaoh
who enslaved the Hebrews
and subjected them to bitter toil.
God had not forgotten his promise, however.
God preserved
the infant Moses
and raised him up to be the leader
who brought God's people
out of bondage and into the land of promise.

Israel became a mighty nation
under King David.
But rivalry and jealousy among his descendants
led to a separation
into two weaker kingdoms,
Israel and Judah;

Bread? or Crumbs?

Israel,
the kingdom to the north with its capital
at Samaria
had only a transient existence.

Mighty Assyria
came down from the north,
destroyed Samaria,
and carried the descendants of Rachel into exile.
The ten tribes disappeared,
never again to be a factor in the history
of God's people.

Salvation history
is traced through the kingdom to the south,
Judah,
with its center at Jerusalem.
Judah too was vulnerable,
the victim of her own failure
to walk in the ways of God.
Mighty Babylon,
another scourge from the north,
threatened the future of God's people.

In that fateful time,
the voice of the prophet Jeremiah announced,
"A voice was heard in Ramah,
wailing and loud lamentation,
Rachel weeping for her children,
for they were no more.

Rachel,
beloved wife of Jacob,
mother of Joseph and Benjamin,
weeping and lamenting as she lay dying,
even as she gave birth
to a son,
became an historical reminder
to Jeremiah
that Rachel still weeps for her children,

The Weeping Rachel

for the descendants of Joseph
who are no more,
scattered by mighty Assyria
and forever gone from the pages of history.

Jeremiah
holds out a vain hope
that the ten tribes might yet be restored,
that Israel might be whole again,
one family
of God's people
joined together in everlasting covenant with God.

The author of Matthew's gospel
finds in this hope of Jeremiah
a prophecy
of the destruction of the children of Bethlehem
by wicked Herod,
who sought to destroy the new born king.

When the wise men from the East
failed to return to Herod
with news of the child
born at Bethlehem,
Herod
in murderous fury
killed all the male children in Bethlehem
two years and younger,
innocent children sacrificed
upon the altar
of man's lust and greed for power.
A savage and wicked deed;
lives ended
at their beginning.
Many, many lives cut short before their time.

Rachel's children sacrificed,
dying instead of the one destined
to be the Savior of us all.
Dying prematurely

that the Son of God might grow to manhood
and fulfill his calling
to die in our place and restore us to God.

Rachel weeping!
Bethlehem's fathers and mothers
stripped of their precious little ones.
Innocent children
murdered because of the insane jealousy
of a power mad king.
What has been the cost to society
from the murder of little ones over the centuries?
Little ones
who might have been a blessing
to all humankind
if they had grown to manhood and womanhood?
Men and women of insight,
of knowledge,
sharing their gifts and talents from God
with all of us?

How have we suffered over the ages
from the loss of little children,
prematurely dead,
victims of the passion, lust and greed
of the unfeeling, heartless men and women of the past
and of the present?
How many children
cut down before their time?
Their great potential from God
forever lost
by premature death?

Can we ever count the sum total of our loss?
No!
Our loss astronomical,
children destroyed,
victims of wicked, venal men and women
whose sensitivities to love and compassion
dulled and perverted
by passion, greed, and lust for power.

The Weeping Rachel

From the beginning
passion and lust for power
have been expressed in wanton murder.
Cain
killed his brother Abel out of jealousy.
This has been the pattern
that has shaped our mentality and our history—
jealousy, strife, war,
bloodshed, murder.
How many of God's children killed before their time?
How many Rachels
weeping
for her children because they were no more?

The Children

Near two thousand years ago,
a child was born
destined to be the Savior of us all.
A child
endangered from birth
by the passions of a wicked king.
That child grew
to manhood,
and by his quality of life
and by his death
left his mark indelibly
imprinted on every one of us.

He escaped the murderer's sword
in childhood,
but he too was wantonly destroyed
as a young man
when his enemies nailed him to a tree,
the victim of man's inhumanity to man.

He lived and died
for all of Rachel's children.
He lived and died

Bread? or Crumbs?

to bring peace,
an end to fratricide and murder,
to war,
to the slaughter of innocents.

He proclaimed love as the way of life
for us and all people;
the love of God,
who loved his creation so deeply
that he gave his beloved Son
that we might be free
from cruel death.

God's beloved Son lived and died
to bring all humanity into harmony in one family,
where God is Lord,
in which all people of every tribe and nation
love and respect one another.
A people whose goal in life is
to enhance the life of every other.

Peace on earth!
An end to the slaughter of innocents.
Down with our Panamas,
our Romanias,
our South Africas,
our murders on the streets of Burbank
and Los Angeles.

Let there be an end to Rachel's weeping
for her children
slain by the murdering Assyrians,
the wicked Herods;
Herods who walk our planet Earth today
in the guise of law and order;
who drop bombs on innocent children
in the name of patriotism.

After eons of time
Rachel still weeps today,

The Weeping Rachel

weeps bitterly
for the thousands, even millions, of children
cut down
before life has hardly begun.
The unborn aborted.
The new born unloved and unwanted;
Victims
of the insatiable appetite of mothers and fathers
for crack, alcohol, and PCP.

Children abused.
Their minds and spirits
forever bearing the scars
inscribed upon them by deviates and perverts.
Victims
of the insensitivity, the perversion
of those to whom God has entrusted their little lives.

How many children die today
before their time
because we did not care enough?
Rachel weeping
for children perverted and corrupted for life
by what they see and hear in us
who are appointed by God
to be their role models
in godliness and righteousness.

Our world,
a dark and bitter place!
Darkened and forever stained by the cruelty
of those
who care not for Rachel's tears.

Near two thousand years ago
light pierced
the darkness of our world.
The light of God shone from heaven.
Love came to earth
infleshed in a babe born in Bethlehem
to Mary and Joseph.

Bread? or Crumbs?

The one we worship today
came from God
to bring peace on earth.
He is here
in word and sacrament
to bring all of Rachel's children together
into one family.
He is here to give birth
to a new people of God.
A people
dedicated to saving today's children
from the fate of Bethlehem's children
near two thousand years ago.

Let us dry Rachel's tears.
Let us follow his example.
Let us love the little children.
Let us catch the vision
of what we can be
and what the world can become
when the love of God
captures our hearts
and becomes the passion of our mind and spirit.

Oh, Rachel!
If we only had the courage
to follow our leader,
your tears would be turned to joy.
Your sorrow to gladness.
Away with hate!
Away with strife!
Away with bitterness, malice, and war!
These are not of God.
Our God is the God of peace and love.
We who are his creation,
born of him in our baptism,
are to love and seek peace for all people.

The Weeping Rachel

Let love, peace, and joy
be the passion
of our commitment today.
If there is hate, malice, bitterness
in our heart,
let them go!
If there is selfishness and pride
at the center of our being
let them go!
If greed, lust, or covetousness are found in us,
let them go!

God's call to his people today is
to wipe away Rachel's tears,
to turn tears into joy
by our love, our kindness,
our generosity and compassion
for every one of Rachel's children.

God's imperative is:
share his gift of love to us
so generously given
in the life of this little child
born at Bethlehem.
Share this gift with one of Rachel's children
on our doorstep
and even to the far reaches of the world today.

Rachel!
Weep no more!
The messenger of God' love and peace
has claimed our hearts forever.
Let us,
strengthened by his grace and power,
follow in the footsteps
our Savior walked,
that his peace and love
be shed abroad
among Rachel's children everywhere.

9

The Lamb of God

The Epiphany of Our Lord

John 1.29–34

The next day he (John the Baptist) saw Jesus coming toward him and declared, "Here is the Lamb of God who takes away the sin of the world! This is he of whom I said, 'After me comes a man who ranks ahead of me because he was before me.' I myself did not know him; but I came baptizing with water for this reason, that he might be revealed to Israel." John testified and said, "I saw the Spirit descending from heaven like a dove, and it remained on him. I myself did not know him, but the one who sent me to baptize with water said to me, 'He on whom you see the Spirit descend and remain is the one who baptizes with the Holy Spirit.' I myself have seen and have testified that this is the Son of God."

Angelica Lutheran Church
Los Angeles, California

The Lamb of God

The language of the Bible is
at times obscure.
Words and phrases used are no longer a part
of our daily experience and vocabulary.
We have been conditioned
by a twentieth century
city culture,
whereas Jesus
and the authors of our Scripture
were conditioned by a rural and pastoral
way of life.

The symbols used by Jesus
and his followers
for teaching spiritual truth are
from the countryside.
When we read the gospels we note
the analogies made:
A sower of seed.
A grain of mustard seed.
Leaven.
A merchant in search of fine pearls.
A net.
The birds of the air.
The lilies of the field.
Moth and rust.
Ravenous wolves.
A lost sheep.
Laborers in the vineyard.

The symbol used in our lesson is
a lamb.
Jesus is the lamb of God.
What meaning does this have for us?
Not much perhaps.
We have never been shepherds.
We have never raised sheep for a living.

The Biblical Background

The background of the symbol is
the Old Testament.
We must know the Old Testament scriptures
to understand what "Lamb of God"
symbolized.
Sheep and shepherds were common
to the people
of Biblical times.

A few examples of sheep
in the spiritual life of God's people are:
"The Lord is my shepherd,"
one of our favorites.
A lamb was sacrificed to celebrate
the Passover,
the great festival of the people of God.
The word of the prophet Isaiah
immortalized by George Friedrich Handel
in the Messiah,
"He shall feed his flock
like a shepherd."
And another, "I saw all Israel
scattered upon the mountains
like sheep without a shepherd."

The New Testament also has its examples:
The parable of the lost sheep.
The false prophets in sheep's clothing.
Jesus identifying himself as
the Good Shepherd.
His followers are likened to sheep.

These are but a few
of many references to sheep and shepherds.
Why was this such an appropriate symbol?
How can we,
who have no personal knowledge of sheep
and shepherds

recover the deeper meaning behind the symbol?
How can we
have a profound understanding of our Scripture
without this knowledge?
How can these symbols
become meaningful to us today?

John the Baptist identified Jesus as
the Lamb of God.
His reference was to the lamb
killed and eaten
on the day of Passover,
the great feast that celebrated
the deliverance of God's people
from bondage in Egypt.

This was the great historical event
in the life of God's people
that created a community
that still exists thousands of years
after the event.

The Hebrews were held in cruel bondage
in the great kingdom of Egypt.
They could not free themselves from this tyranny.
Their God delivered them.
He saved them from extinction.
He provided for their needs in the wilderness.
He brought them together in community.
He led them to the land of promise.
He made of them a great nation.

The celebration of this great event was
Passover.
On the night of their deliverance from Egypt,
the blood of a lamb
was sprinkled on their doorposts.
The angel of death passed over them,
but there was death of the first born son
in every household of Egypt.

A lamb,
without spot or blemish,
was sacrificed and eaten
to commemorate their deliverance.

But more!
The Israelite who ate of the lamb
believed
that he or she was delivered from slavery,
that he or she was a child of God.
As they ate of the lamb,
they shared in the historical event
of deliverance from Egypt.
That saving event by God
became contemporary for them
in the here and now.

The Meaning of the Symbol

This is the profound meaning
behind the lamb of God symbolism
in our New Testament.
Jesus is the Lamb of God,
sacrificed upon the cross
to deliver us
and all people
from our bondage to the destructive forces
of sin and death.

We and all mankind were in bondage,
a bondage more terrible
than the Hebrew people's bondage
in Egypt.
Sin, evil, death more deadly taskmasters
than the Egyptians
with their whips and hard labor.

We are born into a bondage
more terrible
than any taskmaster could inflict upon us.

The Lamb of God

We are powerless and helpless,
unable to set ourselves free.
God came to us in our weakness,
in our helplessness,
in his Son, Jesus,
the One who is the true and only Lamb of God,
whose body was broken
and whose blood was poured out
that we might be delivered
from the trinity of evil
that held us in bondage.

As we celebrate his death for us
in the Sacrament of the Lord's Supper,
we receive
in and through the bread and wine
the Lamb of God
whose body and blood
were broken and shed for our salvation.

We believe and we confess
that Jesus the Christ is truly present.
We partake of him;
we receive him as gift from God.
The author of John's gospel declares,
We eat his flesh,
We drink his blood,
and the messenger of death passes over us.
We have forgiveness,
life and salvation from God.

God does what is impossible for us.
God delivers us from the powers of sin, evil, and death.
We are inventive,
We are self reliant.
We are imaginative.
There is this area of life over which we have no power
or control.
We cannot free ourselves from the terrible taskmasters—
sin, evil, and death.
They resist every effort by the best and the strongest.

Our only hope is in God.
God provides the lamb,
the sacrifice
that delivers us from our powerful and deadly foes.

The Story of Abraham

Let us recall the story of Abraham,
the first of the patriarchs of Israel.
Abraham journeyed
with his son, Isaac, to the land of Moriah,
to Mount Zion,
to offer an appropriate sacrifice to God.
He prepared an altar.
He bound his son, Isaac,
and placed him upon the wood of the altar
for burning.

God is a great God,
a holy God.
Only the first fruits are an appropriate offering
to honor him.
What is a more appropriate offering
than a son,
or a daughter,
or even an only son
to atone for our sin against God?

Isaac was everything to Abraham;
a son born when he and his wife, Sarah,
were old,
beyond the age for child bearing.
Never again could they have a son.
Abraham
made all the preparations to offer
his first and only son
as a sacrifice to God for his unworthiness,
his sin.

God would not let it be so!
God provided a ram,
locked by his horns in a thicket.
The ram became a substitute for
Abraham's only son.
Abraham by his faith in God
becomes the father of all who believe and trust God.

He is the symbol, the type,
of what we cannot do.
We come to God
with our gifts and offerings,
even the best we possess,
hoping to make restitution to God for our sin.
To no avail.
We are powerless and helpless
to accomplish our own deliverance
from the awfulness of the sin and evil we do.
Our gifts and offerings
cannot remove our guilt.
Our deeds and words cannot purchase
eternal life.

Sin and guilt are the taskmasters
that claim our very life
in payment
for our wrongdoing.
We are in jeopardy without hope.
We live in darkness,
blinded by our self-centeredness,
our self-righteousness,
our greed and lust for power.

The Lamb Sacrificed for Us

There is hope.
There is light to lighten our darkness.
God is present.
He provides the sacrifice,
the lamb,

his only Son,
whose death is our deliverance.
"Behold! the Lamb of God,
who takes away the sin of the world."

This is God's word to us today.
His word has meaning
for us
only when the Lamb of God
becomes our Lamb of God.
Jesus Christ is the Savior of the world.
This becomes meaningful,
the motivating force for who we are
and how we live our earthly life
when he is our Savior.

The question:
Have we wrestled deeply,
profoundly and emotionally
with the question,
"Who is my Savior from the trinity of powers
that hold us in bondage—
sin, evil, and death?

Have we experienced the guilt of Abraham?
Guilt
that compelled him
to place his beloved son
upon the altar
as an offering to God
to atone for his sin?

Have we experienced the anxiety of Abraham,
as he placed his only son, Isaac,
upon the altar,
raised the knife to slay him?
A sacrifice to God
who claimed that which was most precious to him?

The Lamb of God

Have we experienced the great relief of Abraham
when God said,
"Do not lay your hand upon the child,
or do anything to him,
for now I know that you fear me,
seeing you have not withheld your son,
your only son,
from me."

Guilt, anxiety, fear.
The emotions that play upon our hearts,
striving within us
when we come as sinners
into the presence of the holy and almighty God.
Guilt, anxiety, fear.
A terrible burden
to everyone who takes God seriously.

Deliverance, redemption, peace.
Beautiful words of healing and promise
from God
to everyone of us who know
that the Lamb of God has been sacrificed.
God offered
his only Son
to deliver us from guilt, anxiety, fear.
To give assurance
to every wounded heart of
deliverance, redemption, peace.

The lamb of God,
God's only Son,
is our deliverance, our redemption, our peace.
By God's grace alone
we belong to the company of the redeemed,
delivered from our bondage
in Egypt.
We have been brought by God's gracious favor
into the land of promise.
The Lamb of God,

Bread? of Crumbs?

our Shepherd,
has brought us over Jordan.
We are at home even now
as we taste
the sweet deliverance of God.

John the Baptist said,
"I saw the Spirit descend
as a dove from heaven
and remain on him.
This is the One who baptizes you in the Holy Spirit."

The Lamb of God has delivered us.
We are free from bondage
from every deadly and destructive power
to be God's people;
to live as Jesus lived in this world,
trusting God implicitly,
loving people tenderly,
for we have been baptized into his Spirit.

The old has become new.
Our allegiance is no longer to the dark forces
of sin and selfishness.
In baptism,
we have put on Christ.
We are alive in God
and God is alive in us.
God breathes into us the breath of life,
and we come alive,
resurrected from the death of sin.
Alive in God
and to the eternal future.

Our allegiance is to God.
He is Lord,
the center of our self.
The Lamb of God has led us out of the wilderness
into the land of promise,
into the joy of sharing our life,

The Lamb of God

our goods, our all,
to bring the glorious good news
of peace and hope and love
to all people.

Baptized into the Spirit!
What a fantastic gift from God.
Empowered
to overcome the forces of sin and evil
that tempt us daily.
Empowered
to be witnesses
to the grace of God in Christ Jesus
to those around us
who contend with these same forces of temptation
every day.
Empowered by God
to do the impossible,
to be a witness to the grace and favor of God
to our family, our friends,
and to the stranger in our life.

Empowered
to feed the hungry,
to clothe the naked,
to shelter the homeless,
to provide balm for healing to the wounded,
to forgive the sinner,
to give the hand of friendship to the enemy,
to be gentle and kind to the cruel,
to turn the other cheek,
to walk the second mile,
to love the unloved,
to be little Christs to everyone
even as Christ is
the Lamb of God to us.

Life in the Spirit is a powerful life,
equipped by God to do the impossible.
Inspired by the Spirit,

Bread? of Crumbs?

we are empowered
to live as the lambs of God in the world.
as Jesus is God's lamb to us.
Sacrificing and sharing
that others may know the Lamb of God
whose body was broken,
whose blood was poured out
to free us from our bondage.

God be with you.
God be in you
this day
and forever
as we celebrate
the Epiphany of our Lord.

10

The Opening Heavens

The First Sunday after the Epiphany

Mark 1.4–11

John the baptizer appeared in the wilderness, proclaiming a baptism of repentance for the forgiveness of sins. People from the whole Judean countryside and all the people of Jerusalem were going out to him, and were baptized by him in the river Jordan, confessing their sins. John was clothed with camel's hair, with a leather belt around his waist, and he ate locusts and wild honey. He proclaimed, "The one who is more powerful than I is coming after me; I am not worthy to stoop down and untie the thong of his sandals. I have baptized you with water; he will baptize you with the Holy Spirit."

In those days Jesus came from Nazareth of Galilee and was baptized by John in the Jordan. Just as he was coming up out of the water, he saw the heavens torn apart, and the Spirit descending like a dove on him. A voice came from heaven, "You are my Son, the Beloved; with you I am well pleased."

Luther Memorial Church
Burbank, California

The Opening Heavens

The opening heavens!
Have we experienced the heavens torn apart?
Skies darkened by thick ominous clouds.
Suddenly a rift in the clouds.
Light breaks through the darkness.
Darkness covering the earth is pierced
by the brilliance of light.
Darkness is no more.

In the beginning
earth was a wasteland—empty, void.
Darkness ruled the surface of the deep.
God said,
"Let there be light!"
The heavens were torn asunder.
Light brightened the earth.
Light with power to create life;
to rouse within the human spirit
faith, hope, love,
peace, and joy.

The Baptism

When were the heavens opened?
When did light dawn for you and for me?
Was it in the wonder
of a new insight?
A solution to a troublesome problem?
Was it in the wonder of
a deep attraction, a dawning love?

Let us go back in our mind's eye
to the day
Jesus
took on form and meaning for us.
To the day when understanding
of the words,
"He has redeemed me,
a lost and condemned creature,"
burst upon our consciousness with compelling force.

That was a moment, a precious moment
beyond forgetting.
Jesus' baptism
was such a moment in his life.
How strange, we say,
that in a moment of time
the man Jesus
became aware of God's purpose for him
in a new and compelling way.

The evangelist Mark writes,
In the moment of his baptism,
the heavens were torn asunder,
the Spirit of God descended.
Jesus perceived
the beckoning hand of God pointing
his way into the future.
He heard
the voice of God calling,
commissioning him
to proclaim the message of salvation
to all people.

Do you recall your baptism?
Not many of us do.
Most of us were infants,
too young to remember that event.
Were the heavens torn asunder
when you were baptized?
They were not for me.

We were not aware
of what was happening to us
when the waters of baptism
were poured upon our brow.
Is there another event in our spiritual experience
that compares to the experience
of Jesus
when he went down into the waters of baptism?

The Opening Heavens

Perhaps confirmation
was such a time.
My confirmation was
a profound spiritual experience
for a young lad of twelve.

I truly believed
I was committing my life to God.
It was the opening of the heavens for me.
God placed his hand upon me.
Placed his hand with such firmness
I could never thereafter
escape or avoid
his call to me.

What was baptism for Jesus?
The evangelist says,
It was the opening of the heavens;
God made known
to Jesus
with power and understanding.
Jesus became aware
in a unique and profound way
the claim God made upon him.

Luke the evangelist writes,
"Jesus grew in wisdom and stature,
in divine and human favor."
He did not know the future,
the secrets of life
from birth or from childhood.
Only when he had grown to manhood
did he begin to think,
to understand,
and to experience as an adult
the role God intended him to fulfill.

Only when he came forth
from the waters of baptism

Bread? or Crumbs?

did he begin to think,
to understand,
and to experience as an adult the will of God
Baptism—
the most powerful,
the most complete
experience of God he had ever known.

The heavens torn asunder!
An awakening to God
in a new and powerful way.
The meaning and purpose of his life
came into focus
as never before.

God became a reality
in an intimate and personal way
such as he had never known.
He had known God.
He was brought up in the traditions
of God's people.

The opening heavens is
the gospel way of saying,
God gripped him,
God took hold of him with a force
that could not be denied.
Faithfully,
obediently,
with joy and enthusiasm,
he stepped forth into a new role,
a new calling,
a new purpose for life.

Baptism
had such power within him that
it could only be describe in the ultimate,
"The heavens were torn asunder;
the Spirit of God descended upon him."
From that point he became in the fullest sense

the Son of God.
From that experience his life unfolded
in a marvelous and total commitment
in consonance
with the will of God.

The Power of Baptism

Baptism
has such power.
Most of us cannot recall our baptism.
We were too young
when the waters of baptism
were poured upon our brow.

Does baptism have meaning for us
as it had for Jesus,
though we have no recollection of that event?
Emphatically "Yes!"
Baptism is the opening of the heavens to us;
the way of God
into our hearts and lives
in a profound and meaningful way.
God is present
in and through the water and the word.
We do not see him.
We do not sense his touch.

When God comes to us,
we can never be the same.
God always comes in all his creative power
at that moment
when the water is poured
and the word is spoken,
"You are my son.
"You are my daughter.
Today I have brought you into life."

At that moment God comes
to transform us

from a little heathen in darkness
into the newborn child of light.
He transforms us from ego-centered beings,
the condition of all of us
at birth;
earth-bound creatures of a world
that would smother us
in darkness and ignorance
of the true God
and of his will
into heaven-bound men and women
whose foremost goal is
to carry forward God's will and purpose
in everything we do.

Baptism
is the opening of the heavens,
the time of planting the seed of God's word
at the very heart of our self.
Baptism
is God binding himself to us
in covenant,
and we being bound by him in life long covenant
to love, serve, and obey him forever.

This binding to God is
both a binding and a loosing.
For we are set free;
We are delivered
from the darkness of ignorance of God,
of superstition,
of the blindness of seeing ourselves
as the only god we need in life.

God made his claim upon us
when the cross of Christ was imprinted
upon our brow.
God has never,
God will never relinquish that claim upon us.

The Opening Heavens

Life,
physical or mental,
and the spiritual life within is to grow
to maturity,
to the fullness of our potential.
Jesus grew physically, mentally,
and in favor with God and with man.
He grew
to a time in life when it became clear
with overwhelming power
that God alone had priority in his life.

The call of God to you and to me is
to grow as Jesus grew.
To grow to that time and place
where the heavens are torn asunder for us,
the darkness pierced by his light,
and we see with the fullest clarity,
his purpose for us in life.

The opening heavens!
How graciously God reveals himself to us;
his will for us in our present
and into the boundless future.
What a privilege,
this highest calling of all,
to be his disciples, his witnesses,
wherever we are
and in whatever we do in life.

We have been baptized into the life,
into the death,
and into the future by our resurrected Lord.
Baptism
is not the history of our past,
but of our present and of our future.
Jesus
truly and fully entered into his ministry
when the heavens opened
and the Spirit of God descended upon him.

So it is to be with us.
Every day we are to live in the power of our baptism.
When Jesus was tested and tried,
when he was discouraged and troubled,
when he was fearful,
he always returned to the experience
of his baptism.
Returned to that basic building block
for faith and hope and love.

What an experience baptism
for him in daily life.
The momentum of that moment
when the heavens were torn asunder
and the Spirit of God descended upon him
carried him ever onward
in his quest to fulfill
the calling to which God had called him.

This is what baptism means to me
and to you
when the heavens are torn asunder,
and God is revealed to us.
When God calls
to a new meaning and purpose in life.

God is not the distant God,
hidden in the far-away heavens.
God rends the heavens.
He comes down.
He enters into our personal experience.
He makes his eternal claim upon us.
He transplants his Spirit into us.
We no longer belong to self.
We forever belong to God.

The Descending Spirit

There is this difference
between our baptism and the baptism of Jesus.
We are baptized as infants.
He as a full-grown man.
He experienced the power of God as an adult
with powers of reason and understanding
that we did not have as an infant.

He experienced
the opening heavens,
the descending Spirit in a new and powerful way.
The first to experience
the baptism by God in the Spirit,
this new way of God communicating and giving himself
to humankind.

He was brought up
in the traditions of Israel—
traditions that had the sanctity of age.
He could not have been baptized
as a child.
Baptism was not a ritual in ancient Israel.

The opening heavens,
the descending Spirit,
breaks with the traditions of the past
and the beginning
of a new tradition—a new way to God.

Long ago God delivered to Abraham
the ritual of circumcision.
The command included the condition,
"Whoever is not circumcised, does not belong
to the company of God's people."
Jesus was born
into this tradition.
In this tradition he grew to manhood.
The tradition was lacking
a ritual for the inclusion of women.

Women were members of the covenant community
only as members
of a household with a male at the head.
The new covenant
changed this condition in a radical way.
The new covenant,
sealed by the baptism of Jesus,
is for every member of the human family,
male and female,
without exception.

The covenant of old was not always
realized in the lives of God's people.
Their history is a history
of rebellion,
of rejecting God.
of idolatry,
the worship of self,
of power and greed.
They repudiated the God of their fathers.

So it was in the life of Jesus.
He knew in part
the will and purpose of God for him.
In baptism,
the heavens were opened.
The will and purpose of God became clear
in a way
he had never known.

The Spirit of God
became the abiding presence in his life
to guide him
in the will of God.
The Spirit came upon him.
The Spirit of truth and power,
The Spirit of wisdom and understanding.
The Spirit of love for God
and for all that God had made.
The Spirit

that made it possible for him to say,
"Not my will,
but your will be done."

This is the Spirit he bequeaths to us.
The Spirit he implants within us at our baptism;
not when we are adults and full of years,
but at the very beginning of our earthly life.

He comes.
The heavens are opened.
The love of God is planted deep within our bosom.
A love that is to grow and flourish
as we mature
into a Christ-like life
where God is supreme,
our all in all.

The direction of life is set.
We are given the intuition of God
in the Spirit
to discern and distinguish
the ways of the world,
the ways of darkness,
from the ways of light—
to the ways of God.
and to know his way for our life.

We are nurtured in the ways of God
from infancy to the grave
in what God desires us to be and to do.
God speaks to us,
he calls us through our baptism daily
as surely as he spoke
to Jesus that day on the banks
of River Jordan.

His word is the word he addressed to Jesus
in that moment of time.
"You are my Son.

Bread? or Crumbs?

You are my daughter.
Today I have brought you to a new birth,
to a new life.
You are mine.
I am yours."

This is life!
This knowledge that we dwell not in darkness,
but in the light of lights.
The heavens are no longer lowering.
We live in a new heaven on earth
while still in our earthly flesh.
The momentum
of the cross of Christ upon our brow
will carry us safely
through all the dangerous paths of this life.

What grace, what power is ours,
to know from our infant years
and through all our years that
we are never beyond the care and love
of our God who said,
"You are my son.
You are my daughter"
the day the cross of Christ was imprinted upon our brow.

11

From Water to Wine

The Second Sunday after the Epiphany

John 2.1–11

On the third day there was a wedding in Cana of Galilee, and the mother of Jesus was there. Jesus and his disciples had also been invited. When the wine gave out, the mother of Jesus said to him, "They have no wine." Jesus said to her, "Woman, what concern is that to you and to me? My hour has not yet come." His mother said to the servants, "Do whatever he tells you." Standing there were six stone water jars for the Jewish rites of purification, each holding twenty or thirty gallons. Jesus said to them, "Fill the jars with water." They filled them up to the brim. He said to them, "Now draw some out, and take it to the chief steward." So they took it. When the steward tasted the water that had become wine, and did not know where it came from (though the servants who had drawn the water knew), the steward called the bridegroom and said to him, "Everyone serves the good wine first, and then the inferior wine when the guests have become drunk. You have kept the good wine until now." Jesus did this, the first of his signs, in Cana of Galilee, and revealed his glory; and his disciples believed in him.

Luther Memorial Church
Burbank, California

From Water to Wine

A wedding
is a time for joy and celebration.
How happy the bride and groom,
the parents,
the kinfolk and friends.
There may even be a tear or two,
a tear of gladness,
not of sorrow and sadness.
Wine
is for celebrations.
It was so in the time of Jesus
and it is so today.

The Wedding at Cana

Once upon a time there was a wedding
at Cana in Galilee.
Jesus was invited
as a relative or friend of the family.
This wedding almost ended in catastrophe.
The steward
in charge of the wedding celebration
had not planned well.
There was not enough wine.
Weddings were different from ours
in their culture.
They usually lasted for seven days.

What to do?
Too late to order a new supply.
Jesus came to the rescue.
He commanded the servants
to fill six large stone jars with water.
Then he commanded them to draw from the jars
and bring to the host.
It was wine!
Very good wine at that.

Bread? or Crumbs?

The story is unique to John's Gospel.
It is an embarrassment
to those who think that wine
should never be served,
not even for a wedding celebration.
Some would explain that the wine
was not real wine,
but grape juice.
Grape juice would ferment and spoil
in the warm climate of Galilee.

Others marvel
at the wonderful powers of Jesus
to turn water into wine.
He changed water into wine
to demonstrate the mighty power of God.
He was able to do this
because he was divine.

Wine is good.
But it must be used judiciously.
It becomes a veritable demon
to those who become addicted.
How strange that Jesus
would perform such a miracle.

It was not a miracle, however.
The author of John's Gospel identifies the event
as a sign.
Signs and miracles are very different.
A miracle is usually defined
as a deed or event
that transcends or even violates the laws of nature.
A sign is directional.
It points to the inner reality of the deed or event.

How then are we to understand this story?
To what does this sign point?
Surely it cannot be taken literally.
It is impossible to convert

water into wine.
The chemistry is not right.

Only as we enter into the thought patterns,
the theology of the writer,
does changing water into wine
become meaningful.
It would seem to be beneath the dignity of Jesus
to enliven a wedding celebration
by converting water into wine.

When we read this story literally,
Jesus becomes a kind of magician
whose mission is to help people out of predicaments
of their own making.
That is not the image of Jesus
portrayed in our gospel.
We worship Jesus
not as a wine maker,
but as our Savior.

Wine and Salvation

What does converting water to wine
have to do with our salvation?
Everything, according to our evangelist.
This event
is a kind of parable,
a symbolic way of telling the gospel.

Jesus is not a wine producer.
He is redeemer.
He is Lord.
Changing water into wine is a symbolic way
of proclaiming
that Jesus has come
to transform sinners into saints.

How difficult, or even impossible, that is.
Sinners are sinners and saints are saints.

Bread? or Crumbs?

Even the most saintly person
acts very unsaintly at times.
The evangelist is telling us how impossible it is
for sinners to transform themselves
into saints.
It is as impossible as changing water into wine.

The most skilled chemist
cannot convert water into wine.
Nor can the most saintly of saints convert
herself or himself into perfection.
Nor can a saint convert a sinner
into sainthood.
This has been tried.
We have known women who have married
to change a man
and vice versa.
But has there ever been success?

Reform, or change,
does not come from within us
by our own effort or strength.
The change from sinner to saint
comes only from God.
God's purpose is always
to transform sinners into saints.
His concern is never with trivialities,
such as changing water into wine
to gladden a wedding party.

Jesus came from God to save sinners,
not to entertain wedding parties.
He called and appointed Jesus at his baptism
to go forth with the good news
that has power to transform sinful humans
into saints.

We can never be the same person
when we have heard
God's good news with our mind and heart.

From Water to Wine

We either respond in faith
or in unbelief.
We are either converted from sinner to saint,
or we are set more firmly
in the cement of our sinnerhood.

An either/or takes place in our heart
when we hear the word of God
We respond in faith or unbelief.
We are never neutral
when the word of God is heard.

Our response
may not be immediately apparent
or visible.
The steward at the wedding feast
did not know
that water had been changed to wine
until he tasted it.

In the same way
we cannot know what change has taken place
in the heart and mind
of those who hear the word of God.
He or she may seem to be the same person,
but only the taste,
that is, our deeds and actions
make known
whether there has been a change.

Our thoughts and attitudes
play decisive roles
in the lives of our family,
our friends and acquaintances,
only as this becomes visible to others
that there has been a dramatic change in us.
The power of God in us
will be sensed by those around us.

Bread? or Crumbs?

Water is good.
It does not bring a new and special dimension
to the wedding celebration.
Wine does.
We are the new wine of God
when the Spirit of God dwells within.
The new "I" radiates gladness and joy
to all who are at the feast.

There is a great multitude
thirsting for God.
searching for a new taste in life,
a new wine.
We who have been changed from water
into wine
can be the new elixir of life for them.
Behold how the multitudes
are in a feverish activity,
seeking security and pleasure.
power and wealth.
They are ignorant that the deep yearnings within
for satisfaction
are a thirst for the living God.

We strive and search for fulfillment.
We create new security blankets
to cover our nakedness
in the presence of the living God.

We find them not.
There is so much water out there
and so little wine;
so many shallow Christians
without a deep, abiding commitment
to the Creator God.

Where are the people of God
who are aflame with passion for righteousness,
for justice,
with zeal and enthusiasm

that can move mountains?
with love and compassion for the poor
and downtrodden?

Are we examples of
water changed into wine?
Are we sinners transformed into saints?
Do we come to the wedding feast,
but never enter into the celebration?

The New Religion

Our transformation
from water to wine
will be evident in who we are,
in what we think and do and say.
When we are the true wine of God,
the taste will be in the mouths of all
who share in the quality of our life
as we associate
and fellowship with them
in our home,
at our place of work,
and in every relationship of life.

The true state of our heart,
our mind and spirit,
is plainly evident
when we have become new wine
through the grace of God.

Wine must be tasted
to determine its quality.
Christians are to be seen and heard.
Only genuine wine makes an impression
upon those who taste it
as they share with us
in every relationship of life.

Bread? or Crumbs?

Saints of God!
Let the transformation be known.
Bear witness to the One who has changed you
from sinner to saint
in your thoughts, words and deeds.
Saints of God!
Lead the celebration of life at the wedding feast
by the direction of your life,
by your life style,
by the meaning and purpose of your life
tasted by others.

Water in the parable
represents the old time religion,
the religion of the fathers,
the Old Testament religion
of laws and rules, a religion
sacred with age.

What is the problem with the old?
Much in every way.
If God could have saved all humanity
with the Old Testament religion,
he would not have needed
to send his Son to change water into wine.

Jesus came from God
to change the old relationship
of law and obedience
into a new relationship of faith and love;
a relationship
founded upon the grace and mercy of God,
not upon a pseudo piety,
a pseudo obedience,
a pseudo goodness.
A radical change from the boast of the proud Pharisee
who in the temple,
in the very presence of God, prayed,
"I thank you that I am not as other people."
Is this prayer?

From Water to Wine

It is the pleading of the tax collector,
who stood at a distance,
who smote his breast
with head bowed down.
Who cried,
"God, be merciful to me,
a sinner."

We come to the wedding celebration,
unaware that the old wine
is deadly,
poisoning our relationship with God
and with one another.

God serves a new wine
at his wedding feast.
A wine that is life-giving,
a wine that builds an eternal structure
of integrity and humility,
of righteousness and truth,
of kindness and love,
of generosity and sincerity
in the minds and hearts of all who partake,
who drink deeply
of this life giving beverage
drawn from the deep vessels
of God's eternal compassion and love.

God has saved this good wine until now.
We are blessed,
not because we are more deserving
than those of old,
but because there was need
to build to this new level of understanding
step by step
over the eons of time.

What have we done?
We crucified the wine bearer.

Bread? or Crumbs?

We subjected him to humiliation,
to a cruel death,
because change can only come at great cost
to those
who initiate a radical departure from the past.

What do we do even now?
We who have tasted so freely of the new wine.
Have we not changed God's wine back into water
with our prejudices,
our indifference to others,
our exclusion of many from the wedding celebration,
our majoring in the trivialities of religion?

Is Jesus at our celebration today?
Yes, he comes in word and sacrament,
still offering the life-giving wine
that saves from sin and death.
He comes to change us
from our old ways into the new.

He comes to give flavor,
quality and depth to our understanding of God,
to our commitment to him.
A flavor, a quality
that distinguishes us,
the new from the old,
even as the wine at Cana was distinguished
from the water poured into
and drawn from the vessels for purification
at the door of the wedding feast.

He comes
to change our religion of self-satisfaction
and self-importance
into an enthusiastic, persevering service
of all of God's creation,
for all of God's creatures,
and above all
of God's people on the face of Planet Earth.

From Water to Wine

He comes
to awaken us and to quicken us to a new life,
to become God's hands and feet and voices
wherever we are.
He comes
to plant deep within our bosom
a vision
of who we can be and what we can do
to transform all humanity
and all the environment
into the new wine of God.
To bring all humanity together
into one community
where each seeks the good
of every other.

We hear the word today.
We learn from this word what is God's will for us.
Do we remain empty jars, useless,
stagnant,
empty of the positive,
filled with all the negatives
of seeking our own in everything we do,
even in God?

Or are we the new wine,
the wine of God,
so that the pages we write day by day
in our book of life
are read and heard by all
who seek in and through us
the way to God?

12

In the Power of the Spirit

The Third Sunday after the Epiphany

Luke 4.14–21

Then Jesus, filled with the power of the Spirit, returned to Galilee, and a report about him spread throughout all the surrounding country. He began to teach in their synagogues and was praised by everyone.
When he came to Nazareth, where he had been brought up, he went to the synagogue on the sabbath day, as was his custom. He stood up to read, and the scroll of the prophet Isaiah was given to him. He unrolled the scroll and found the place where it was written:
"The Spirit of the Lord is upon me,
because he has anointed me
to bring good news to the poor.
He has sent me to proclaim release to the captives
and recovery of sight to the blind,
to let the oppressed go free,
to proclaim the year of the Lord's favor."
He rolled up the scroll, gave it back to the attendant, and sat down. The eyes of all in the synagogue were fixed on him. Then he began to say to them, "Today this scripture has been fulfilled in your hearing."

Luther Memorial Church
Burbank, California

In the Power of the Spirit

"Jesus,
filled with the power of the Spirit
returned to Galilee."
How do we define or describe "Spirit"?
Spirit is mysterious.
Spirit is called "the breath of life" in Scripture,
the life principle.
How difficult it is for us to find words
to describe or to define
the life principle.

How is it that the ancients equated
spirit and breath?
In ancient Hebrew,
"Spirit" is called *ruach*.
Ruach has a double role,
for *ruach* is also the word for wind or breath.

In similar fashion in ancient Greek,
the word for spirit, wind and breath is
pneuma.
We recognize that word in our language
in the words pneumatic and pneumonia.

Why did the ancients use the same word
for breath, wind, and spirit?
Perhaps because there is something mysterious
about wind, breath, and spirit.
We feel the presence of wind and breath,
although we cannot see them.
We cannot hold them in our hand.
This is a mystery,
since they are a reality but intangible.

We are alive.
We breathe.
When we inspire or breath,
we are alive, living beings.

When breath goes forth from us at our last moment.
when we expire,
we are dead.

This is a mystery beyond comprehension,
or description.

In the beginning
God shaped our bodies
out of the dust of the ground.
Then God breathed into that body of dust
the breath of life
and we became human.
We came alive.
This word of God teaches us
that in our deepest essence
we are human
when we are inspired, inbreathed,
inspirited by the breath of God.

Jesus, Filled with the Spirit

Jesus began his ministry
in the power of the Spirit.
He said,
"The Spirit of the Lord is upon me."
His deeds and words demonstrated
the presence and power of the Spirit.
From whence did the Spirit come to him?

We shared in the word of God two weeks ago
that the Spirit
descended upon him when he was baptized.
At that moment
God inbreathed Jesus.
God inspired him
to become the Savior of all mankind,
to bring salvation,
the life in the Spirit, to all humanity.

In the Power of the Spirit

Jesus came in the power of God;
not in his own power.
He came in the power of the Spirit,
inbreathed by God.

How mysterious the story
of God's creation of man and woman.
He breathed into a lump of clay
and Adam became a living spirit.
How mysterious the story
of God's choosing Jesus
out of the entire human family
to be the one
through whom salvation comes to all people.

How mysteriously God works.
He breathes into us,
he inspirits us
as the waters of baptism are placed upon our brow
and we come alive in the Spirit.
God inbreathed us
in that moment of time when the waters of baptism
were splashed upon us.
At that moment you and I became a child of God,
no longer a creature
shaped and molded from dust,
but shaped and molded in the image of our Father God.

How mysterious the event
when God chooses from among us
the ones to be prophets,
proclaimers of his word.
The mystery is beyond our powers to explain.

All this is as mysterious as the wind that blows
and the breath we breathe.
We sense and feel the wind and the breath.
We know their presence.
It is like Jesus said to Nicodemus,
"The wind blows where it chooses;

you hear the sound of it,
but you do not know where it comes from
or where it goes.
So is everyone who is born of the Spirit."

We see the leaves stirring in the breeze,
the grass gently waving,
the eddying dust,
the waves pounding on the shore.
We know the power of the wind
in tornado and hurricane.
We cannot hold the wind or breath in our hand.
We cannot examine them with our eye.

Wind is one of the many gifts from God.
Without wind earth would be barren,
unwashed by rain;
earth without life,
and we could not be.

God alone appoints and chooses
the ones whom he desires to be prophets,
his spokesmen and spokeswomen,
bringing his message of truth,
of love and hope
to all that he has inbreathed
with the breath of life.

There is a calling from God for each of us,
a vocation to fulfill
to serve one another,
using the special gifts God has entrusted
to each one of us
when he inbreathed us with the breath of life.
Your calling and mine
are special,
for inscribed upon each one of us is
the handwriting of God who wrote,
"You are mine.
I have inbreathed you and inspired you

In the Power of the Spirit

to use your special gifts
to serve one another faithfully
according to your talents."

There is nevertheless the mystery.
Sometimes the calling of one seems more special
than the calling of another.
When we see the total picture,
it becomes clear that each one of us has a special calling,
whether it be teaching,
governing, manufacturing, merchandising,
transporting, food preparation,
cleaning, care giving.
For we are dependent upon one another.
It is like the web of nature,
where all plants and animals are dependent
upon one another for life and survival.

The Spirit came upon Jesus at his baptism.
His calling was special in a special way.
The Spirit empowered him
to proclaim good news to the poor,
to announce freedom for the captives,
to give sight to the blind,
to set free the oppressed,
to announce the year of the Lord's favor.
In the same way,
but in different capacities the Spirit empowers
each one of us
to fulfill God's special role for you and for me
in our special calling.

The Spirit and Life

We are inbreathed,
we are inspirited by the breath of God,
else we are not human.
God's inbreathing distinguishes us
from all creatures.
How tragic

that a great multitude destined to be human,
destined to be empowered by the Spirit of God,
live below the level of true and authentic humanity,
using their gifts and talents
to deny the handwriting of God upon them.

How many reject the qualities of love,
truth, goodness, trust,
honesty, faithfulness,
the qualities of the truly human
inbreathed by the breath of God.

We fall below the level of genuine humanity
whenever the Spirit of God
is not reflected
in who we are
and in what we think and do and say.
We have been baptized in the Spirit.
God has inspirited us.
God has placed his Spirit within us.

Nevertheless we can live below the level
of the inbreathed life.
When our deeds and words are motivated by
selfishness and self-interest,
when we manifest a mean, unforgiving spirit,
when we deceive, lie, and steal,
when we blaspheme and gossip,
when we covet and lust,
when we hate or despise another,
we are denying the One who has created us,
who has inbreathed us
with his life giving Spirit.

We think and act in this way
when we have let the spirit of darkness
take possession
of our spirit,
overriding the Spirit God implanted within us
when he said,

In the Power of the Spirit

"You are mine.
You belong to no other."

Inbreathed by the breath of God,
we are transformed into Christ-likeness.
We are Christian.
We bear his name not upon our shirtsleeve,
but deep within our very bosom.
We are truly human,
as Jesus was human in the highest sense
of that word.

We are the believing, trusting, loving
people of God,
living as God would have us live
in the world,
untainted by the temptations
to go our own way,
to do our own thing,
to deny the gifts of the Spirit
that God has fashioned within us.

Who was Jesus
before the Spirit of God came upon him
in this new and powerful way?
Jesus was a carpenter.
Carpenters fulfill a very necessary role
in our society.

Carpenters are skilled mechanics
who build houses
and furnish them.
Who build churches and our capitol buildings.
Who create and form
great and beautiful structures housing
our business and our industry.

Jesus was a carpenter,
a necessary and God-given vocation.
God had another and a different calling

Bread? or Crumbs?

for this carpenter from Galilee.
At the fullness of life
he was baptized.
The heavens opened,
God breathed upon him.
The Spirit came upon him with power.

God chose this carpenter
and set him apart
to build a new structure,
a new community
that God called "My Church."

The Church,
the body of believers inbreathed
by this same Spirit of God.
God's people
fashioned out of rude clumps of clay
made fully and truly human
through the inbreathing of the breath of God.

Lumps of clay
set free from discontent and selfishness,
from the chains of darkness and evil,
free from ignorance and immorality,
free to be shaped and molded
by the hand of God
into a new people—God's holy people.

Jesus came forth
from the waters of baptism
inbreathed by the breath of God.
He went forth
into the world in the power of the Spirit
to proclaim good news,
"Every slave is freed from bondage
to all that is not God."

Carpentering prepared him
to build the Church of God.

In the Power of the Spirit

He said,
"The Spirit of the Lord is upon me.
He has anointed me to preach good news,
release to captives,
sight to blind eyes,
freedom for the oppressed.
This is the year of the Lord's favor."

What a transformation!
How marvelous the power of the Spirit,
to transform a simple carpenter
into the architect
to become the Savior of the world.

Our Calling

Whatever our vocation in life—
carpenter, sales person,
teacher, homemaker, clerk,
accountant, nurse, manager, pilot,
counselor, engineer, farmer—
our calling is from God
who has placed his imprimatur of blessing upon us.

We are called by the Spirit of God in us
to live up to the highest expectations
for our calling
to the glory of God.

But more—
to know that in our baptism
when God breathed into us the breath of life,
he gave to us a higher calling
to be his man,
his woman, his child in life.
Anointed to proclaim good news
of the inspirited life
wherever we are
and to whomever we meet.

Bread? or Crumbs?

There is a great multitude out there
living in spiritual poverty
below the level of authentic humanity.
Living in fear, anxiety and distress.
Living in ignorance, prejudice, and distrust.
Living in bitterness, malice, envy, and jealousy.
Living in greed, suspicion, and dishonesty.
Lives corrupted and deformed
because they have not heard,
or have not heeded, the good news
that God is present
in Jesus the Christ
to set them free from all
that binds them to mortality and meaninglessness.

God has anointed us with his Spirit.
We are free
from all the powers of evil and darkness
that corrupt and destroy.
Free by the grace of God
to live on a higher plane.
Free to announce to the world fearlessly
the great glad news
to all who know not God
that he is here to inbreath them too
and to implant within them his Spirit.

We are to be like the wind,
mysteriously moving
among those who know not God,
bringing the breath of life to the dead.
We are to be a powerful wind,
blowing upon all
who are groveling in the filth of wickedness,
raising them up
to a life of hope, peace and joy.

We are to proclaim release to those
enslaved to passion and lust,
to wealth and pleasure.

In the Power of the Spirit

We are the breeze of God,
a gentle but powerful wind
breaking the fetters of the oppressed,
raising them from hopelessness and despair
to a life of service
in the community of God's people everywhere.

Jesus came preaching
and the fetters fell;
lives changed, transformed by the Spirit—
fishermen, tax collectors,
housewives, sinners,
even harlots.
Inbreathed by the breath of God,
became a new people.

Inspired by the Spirit,
they went forth with good news,
as their beloved Lord Jesus had gone before them.
The life style of many was changed,
even as they themselves had been changed,
as they shared the good news
of God's grace with others.

They made a mighty impact for righteousness
upon the ungodly.
The walls of injustice and tyranny
came tumbling down,
as they lived and proclaimed their faith.

Blind eyes were opened.
Ignorance and superstition changed
into knowledge of God.
Men and women demoralized and corrupted
by fear, anxiety, and brutishness
were invigorated by the breath of God
to live holy and righteous lives
in the midst of the world.

Bread? or Crumbs?

What power belongs to the life in the Spirit.
Power to give sight to the blind.
Power to lift the curtain of darkness
shrouding the lost,
separating them from the light of the world,
Jesus our Messiah.

Jesus,
filled with the power of the Spirit,
went forth in the name of God to proclaim
the Good News of life from death,
of light from darkness,
of love from hate,
of peace from strife.
His Spirit is among us,
to speak this powerful word of God.

What is our calling in life?
Our callings are as diverse as the individuals among us.
carpenters, electricians, plumbers,
bookkeepers, secretaries,
merchants, mechanics,
bankers, financial advisors,
doctors, nurses, students,
truckers, entertainers, photographers.

One calling we have in common—
to tell the good news
of the gospel
by our words, our deeds,
our personal discipline and personal habits,
by our prayers and our conversation.

Jesus came in the power of the Spirit.
The breath he breathed,
the words he spoke,
the deeds he did,
set in motion powerful forces
that still move among us today.

In the Power of the Spirit

He lived and walked among us
and we became the people of God,
commissioned to do in our day
what he and his disciples did in their day.
We are the breath of God
breathing upon one another
and upon all the children of men and women around us.

What happened in century one
can only happen in century twenty-one
when we faithfully
and joyfully
go forth in the power of the Spirit
to touch the lives of many
as we breathe upon them the breath of God.

There will be renewal.
There will be transformation.
There will be life from the dead
as the gospel
in word and song
sounds forth wherever we are.
As our hands reach out in love and kindness
and our feet trod the pathways of peace.
Let us believe and act,
for God has breathed upon us today.

13

Blessed are the Pure in Heart

The Fourth Sunday after the Epiphany

Matthew 5.1–10

When Jesus saw the crowds, he went up on the mountain; and after he sat down, his disciples came to him. Then he began to speak, and taught them, saying:
"Blessed are the poor in spirit,
for theirs is the kingdom of heaven.
Blessed are they who mourn,
for they will be comforted.
Blessed are the meek,
for they will inherit the earth.
Blessed are those who hunger and thirst
for righteousness
for they will be filled.
Blessed are the merciful,
for they will receive mercy.
Blessed are the pure in heart,
for they will see God.
Blessed are the peacemakers,
for they will be called children of God.
Blessed are those who are persecuted
for righteousness' sake,
for theirs is the kingdom of heaven."

Luther Memorial Church
Burbank, California

Blessed are the Pure in Heart

From ancient times
it was believed that
the heart
was the center of emotions.
We reason with our minds.
We feel with our hearts,
We act in and through our bodies.
It is probably more correct to say,
The total person is involved
at every moment
in thinking, feeling, or doing.

When I lift my hand to my brow,
my entire person is involved—
my mind, my body, and my spirit.
The person is not a collection of parts.
The person is more than the sum total
of body, mind, and soul.

Emotions, or feelings,
are not the sum total of a personality.
Thoughts
are not the sum total of a personality.
Deeds
are not the sum total of a personality.

You and I exist only
in the unity of our body, our mind, and our soul.
This trinity always functions together as one.
A body cannot exist by itself,
A mind cannot exist by itself.
A spirit, or soul, cannot exist by itself.

We confess in our faith,
"I believe in the resurrection of the body."
That is why it is wrong, when we say,
"When I die,
my soul goes to heaven."

Bread? or Crumbs?

According to the faith we confess,
the total person is
asleep in the grave until the trumpet sounds.

Nevertheless,
it may be meaningful
to consider
that aspect of our personhood
we call our affections.
Let us consider our heart to be the center
of our emotional being.

Our heart experiences love,
desire,
sorrow and anguish,
friendship and loneliness,
joy and gladness.
Jesus said that the heart is the source of
evil thoughts and desires,
evil words and deeds.
Out of the heart issue
passion and lust,
greed and pride,
hatred and selfishness.

An honest and good heart is
a heart
that has been changed radically
by God.
The Psalmist wrote,
"Create in me a clean heart, O God."
He acknowledged
how deeply the heart is involved
in sinful acts and attitudes.
Then the Psalmist prays for a new heart.

Jesus said to his disciples,
"Blessed are the pure in heart,
for they shall see God."
Who are the pure in heart?

Blessed are the Pure in Heart

Are they the ones who have never sinned?
or do not sin?
The Psalmist confesses in the same psalm,
"I was brought forth in iniquity,
and in sin did my mother conceive me."

We are sinners from the beginning of life,
not that we have committed a thought or act
that is sinful,
but because we are born into
a human family
that by nature is self-centered,
not God-centered.
The pure in heart are those whose hearts
are God–centered.

The writer of the Epistle of John wrote,
"If we say we have no sin,
we deceive ourselves
and the truth is not in us."

If we do not live under the discipline of God,
we are self-centered and selfish,
seeking our own in everything we do,
even in God.
As we grow in years,
we become more selfish,
more ingrown,
more contrary to God
in what we think, and do, and say.

Our deepest need from birth to death,
as the author of our gospel writes, is
purity of heart.
At the beginning of life
when we were most helpless,
God came to cleanse us of our impurity,
to give us a pure heart.
He came in the waters of baptism
to make us clean,
to give us a pure heart.

We were washed,
we were cleansed as the water of baptism
touched our brow,
and that water
was joined with the powerful word of God.

The pure in heart
are those of any age:
The infant child born again in baptism.
The youth, the middle-aged,
and even the elderly
who are sanctified and made holy
by that rite of baptism,
when the water is joined to the word of God.
We, the baptized,
are the pure in heart.
This is the indicative.

And now the imperative.
We, who have been baptized,
are to be pure in heart in our thoughts,
our words, and our deeds.
The Apostle Paul writes
to the Christians at Rome,
"Do not let sin reign in your mortal bodies."

There is always this conflict within—
the old nature we have from our physical birth,
and the new nature born in us through baptism.
We live in these two worlds
as long as we are in the flesh.
That is why Luther wrote in his Catechism,
"Our old nature must be drowned and destroyed
by daily sorrow and repentance,
and the new nature come forth daily
to live for God."

We live in a hostile world,
a world whose values and goals

are always in conflict
with the values and goals of our baptized life,
for, as the Apostle has written,
we are not to let sin reign in our mortal bodies.
Our Lord calls us
to a life of purity.
We are confronted by the world's symbols
that constantly suggest and lead us
to evil thoughts and deeds.
A beautiful woman,
clothed in scanty attire,
a sex symbol,
the inducement to sell hundreds of products:
from toothpaste to Pepsicola,
from beer to cars,
clothing,
and even homes.
How difficult to be pure in heart.

Woman,
the crown of God's creation,
the mother of our children,
defiled and profaned by the world around us.
Do we wonder why sex crimes,
abuse and rape
are so common in our society?

The pure in heart
are not free from temptation.
The pure in heart wrestle with temptation daily.
Only as we walk humbly
with our God
in prayer and in the daily nourishment
of his word,
can we be freed from this terrible temptation
to become like the world
by repudiating purity of heart.

"The love of money,"
says Scripture,

Bread? or Crumbs?

"is the root of all kinds of evil."
The temptation is always with us
to strive for wealth
no matter the cost to our brother and our sister.

There is gross dishonesty
even by those who appear to be pure in heart.
Cheating, stealing, fraud
are practiced without a twinge of conscience
by many who present a sanctimonious front
to the world.
April fifteenth
is such a day for many "honest" people.
It has been estimated
that more than a hundred billion dollars
is never collected annually.
How many church members partake
in this form of duplicity,
this cheating?

The temptation is with us daily,
we the pure in heart,
to fudge,
and even to be outright deceitful
in reporting our income.
"Many get away with it,
so why should not I?"
we say.

The love of money
is a terrible taskmaster,
rearing its ugly head in many guises.
We, the pure in heart,
wrestle with this temptation constantly.
Honesty and integrity
are marks of a pure heart.
Our purity
can only be maintained
when we are in an abiding relationship
with our God.

We live in the world.
We are exposed to many and various temptations.
The Apostle wrote
to the saints in the church at Corinth,
"Do not let the world squeeze you
into its mold."
Do not let your values and ideals
be shaped
by the sham values
of a pagan society.

"Let the word of God dwell in you richly,"
wrote the Apostle.
The Bible
stills tops the list of bestsellers
in our bookhouses.
Too often the Bible
is like a sacred charm to many,
an amulet to ward off evil,
for we scarcely use it.

Purity of heart does not grow
through proximity to a sacred book.
The message of the book
must be grafted into our hearts
by regular and diligent use.
Sad to say,
the only exposure to the word of God
for many church members is
the reading of the lessons
at the Sunday worship
and a ten to fifteen minute exposition
of that word in the sermon.

Seldom do we have a gathering of the family
around the word of God
for devotions and prayer
that was the daily practice by families
a generation or two ago.

We do not practice this wonderful time together,
because we are so seldom together.

Do we wonder why there are troubled,
dying churches?
Why there is a continuing decline
in membership
among the main line churches?

Purity of Heart

We can be pure in heart only
when we rely upon our daily conversation with God
in prayer
and in searching the Scriptures.
"Abide in me, and I in you,"
said Jesus.
"As the branch cannot bear fruit of itself,
unless it abides in the vine,
neither can you, unless you abide in me."

We are called and chosen by God
to be pure in heart,
models in this world of impurity and unholiness.
We cannot be pure in our own strength.
The pressures of the world
are tremendous daily.
Peer pressure from well-meaning friends
test us daily
to compromise the values and ideals
we have from our Lord.

How can we be pure in heart?
Only when we are in close fellowship with God.
Only as there is a serious commitment
to prayer
and the study of God's word.

The word of God today,
"Blessed are the pure in heart,

Blessed are the Pure in Heart

for they shall see God,"
is a reminder
that there is a way to be pure in heart,
and a wonderful promise to all
who are steadfast and true to this commitment.
The entry is narrow
and the way is hard.
It is that daily reliance upon
the God of our salvation.
It is the discipline of walking humbly
with our God.
How marvelous the promise
to those who persevere,
"You shall see God."
God is very present to us
in our daily struggle with the realities of life
in the world around us.

There is much that is ugly
in the world around us.
As I drove to Long Beach Wednesday
to see Dutch,[1]
I was appalled at the smog
hanging over the freeway.
A smog so heavy
it obscured the street signs at times.
I brought Dutch pictures
of Minnesota lakes
and Yosemite mountains and waterfalls.
"How clean and beautiful it looks,"
said Dutch.

Often we cannot see God
through the smog that shrouds
are minds and hearts,

---

1. Dutch was in the Veterans' Hospital, totally immobilized and helpless, a victim of a polio epidemic in an Army camp in Texas years earlier. At the inception of the disease, Dutch was in an iron lung for a long period of time. The attitude of Dutch was amazing. He said, "When the Lord brought me into this world, he never promised me more than I am." His attitude and his faith were amazing.

BREAD? OR CRUMBS?

because the world is too much with us.
"Blessed are the pure in heart,"
said Jesus,
"for you shall see God."

We see him in the Planet Earth around us,
created by God in all its beauty,
untainted by man's greed and thoughtlessness.
We see him in the glorious sunrise,
holding forth the promise of a new day of grace,
filled to the brim with the presence of God.

We see him
in the flower and in the tree,
in the clear sparkling water,
in the mountain
and on the plain.
We see him
in the flight of the tanager,
the squirrel darting up the tree.
the little chipmunk with its merry ways.
We see him
in the little child's dimpled smile,
in the peace and contentment on the face
of our aged grandfather.
We see him
in these and many places,
when we are the pure in heart,
our hearts in tune with our Maker
and our God.

We see him
in the expressions of kindness and love
of those surrounding us,
our dear family and our friends.
We see him
in the little child,
so trusting,
so open and eager to partake of all
in range of her vision.

Blessed are the Pure in Heart

We see God here
when our hearts are pure,
in tune with the God of Word and Sacrament.

We see him
in the dying Jew alongside the roadside,
a victim of the greed of a brother,
tended by a stranger,
a Samaritan,
who was anathema to Jews.
We see him
in the homeless and the hungry
we are called to feed and shelter.
We see him
in the multitudes who are like sheep
without a shepherd,
brought up in ignorance and superstition
without knowledge of the true God.
We see him
in the unbeliever,
sometimes turned off by the arrogance
and self-righteousness
of those who boast of their status with God.

We see him
in all of these places and more
when we are in tune with the living God,
the maker of heaven and earth.
We see him
when we are moved profoundly
by his acts of grace to us
in the moments of our deepest need.
We see him,
we, the pure in heart,
purified and sanctified by the forgiving touch
of our God upon our brow.

We see him,
when we are in a deep and abiding relationship
with him

through the graciousness of his Son,
our Lord Jesus,
who bore our sin upon the tree
to set us free
from its dread consequences,
death and eternal doom.

As we travel
the pathways of life,
we become like the one
who commands our heart's affection.
When our life
is centered in the living God,
we will see him,
we will become like him—
gentle, compassionate, loving,
gracious, forgiving,
a leaven working
in the dough of this world
to bring peace and joy and love
to the wounded hearts around us.

This is our prayer,
our goal,
to become like him.
His promise is greater than we can ever
imagine,
"Blessed are the pure in heart,
for they shall see God."

14

The Dot and the Iota

The Fifth Sunday after the Epiphany

Matthew 5.17–20

"Do not think that I have come to abolish the law and the prophets; I have not come to abolish but to fulfill. Truly I tell you, until heaven and earth pass away, not one letter, not one stroke of a letter, will pass from the law until all is accomplished. Therefore, whoever breaks one of the least of these commandments, and teaches others to do the same, will be called least in the kingdom of heaven; but whoever does them and teaches them will be called great in the kingdom of heaven. For I tell you, unless your righteousness exceeds that of the scribes and Pharisees, you will never enter the kingdom of heaven."

St. Andrew Lutheran Church
Andrews, North Carolina

The Dot and the Iota

The dot.
Smallest letter in the Hebrew alphabet.
A marking inserted within,
under, or above a consonant
to indicate the vowel sound.
The Hebrew language is consonantal.
Only consonants are written.
The reader
supplies the proper vowel
to form the syllable and the word.

With the passage of time,
when Jews were forced to use Aramaic
as the official language,
they lost reading skills in Hebrew.
Vowels were supplied;
a system of dots and dashes devised
to supply the correct vowels to the consonants.

The iota.
The smallest letter in the Greek alphabet.
The iota is a vowel,
the equivalent of our letter "i."

Hebrew
was the language of the ancient Scriptures,
the Torah, the Prophets, and the Writings.
We call this book The Old Testament.

Greek
was the language of the later Scriptures,
and of our New Testament.

Jesus said,
"Heaven and earth will pass away,
but not an iota,
not a dot,
will pass from the law
until all is accomplished."

Bread? or Crumbs?

Jesus said,
Scripture stands forever!
Scripture is the unwavering testimony
to the purpose of God.
God is holy,
majestic, almighty,
creator of heaven and earth.

The Scripture

God has made known his will
that we be righteous and holy,
without sin.
We are called to give up every sin,
even our favorite sins.
Who does not sin?
Who has the strength and will power
not to sin?
We sin
even when we strive not to sin.

Our thoughts, words, and deeds
are tainted by pride,
prejudice, and selfishness.
Luther wrote,
"There is not a thing we do
for which we do not need to ask forgiveness."
God comes in Jesus the Christ
to free us from this bondage.
He comes to plant within us a new Spirit,
a loving, magnanimous spirit,
freed from pride, prejudice, and selfishness.

Our freedom comes at great cost.
"God loved the world so much
that he gave his only Son."
Freedom from sin is
a priceless gift shared freely with us.
The Gospel is "good news,"
God's declaration

that he has come and he comes now
to set us free from our bondage to sin.

Jesus said,
"Not a dot, not an iota,
will pass from the law until all is accomplished."
God has taken a stance against sin;
against gross sins and against sins
we consider to be of little consequence.
Jesus came
to make known God's implacable posture
against sin.
But more,
to make known God's unswerving love
for the sinner.

Illustrations and Examples

There were those who heard Jesus proclaim
the love of God,
who responded with joy.
They received him as God's messenger.
They believed him.
They received a new and precious gift
from God—
freedom from their bondage to sin.

There were others who rejected him
and his message.
The truth of what he said
laid bare the hypocrisy,
the self-righteousness,
the pride and malice
that dominated their hearts and thoughts.

They crucified him
to silence the accusing voice.
They believed in their rightness,
that they truly served God
with their piety, their rituals, and sacrifices.

Sin is like that:
devious, blinding the eye and the mind
to truth.
Translating the will and the word of God
into thought patterns
and ways of life
that are pleasing to the inner self,
but unpleasing to God.

Jesus teaching was a threat to tradition,
to the religion of the fathers
they were committed to defend.
Jesus said,
"You have heard that it was said,
'You shall not kill.'
I say to you,
The one who is angry with his brother,
The one who calls another a fool,
The one who shows contempt for another,
has violated the commandment,
'You shall not kill.'"

Jesus said,
"You have heard that it was said,
'You shall not commit adultery.'
I say to you,
The one who lusts,
that is, the one who cultivates sexual desire
in his or her heart,
has violated the commandment."

Jesus said,
"You have heard that it was said,
'You shall not swear falsely.'
I say to you,
The one who speaks a word
that is not trustworthy,
has violated the commandment."
Our 'Yes' or our 'No'
are sufficient when we are an honest person,
a person of integrity.

The Dot and the Iota

Jesus said,
"You have heard that it was said,
'You shall love your neighbor
and hate your enemy.'
I say to you,
Love your enemy.
Love the very one who hates you,
and seeks to destroy you."
What astounding words!
"Love your enemy!"

Jesus words threaten
our peace of mind and heart.
He internalizes and personalizes sin
in a way that casts guilt upon us,
no matter how self-righteous and pious we are.
To live by the commandment
and anticipate our rightness with God
through obedience
is not the way to salvation.

How simple the Christian life,
if all we have to say is,
"I have never killed anyone,"
meaning
"I have never shed blood."

Or to say,
"I have never committed adultery,"
meaning
"I have never had sexual relations
outside of marriage."

Or to say,
"I have never sworn falsely,"
meaning
"I have never violated my oath or my word.
I have always been truthful,
although I haven't always told the whole truth."

Or to say,
"I have always loved my neighbor,"
meaning
"I love my family and my friends,
and I really have no enemies."

We are probably all of us like the elderly lady
in Dostoyevsky's
Brothers Karamazov,
who said to Dimitri,
"I love everyone."
To which Dimitri replied,
"Perhaps someday you may really love someone."

Jesus always creates great discomfort
in the hearts and minds
of all of us who simplify
the commandments of God
and make them to be the essence of the godly life.
He went to the heart of our conduct,
our motivation.
Why do we do what we do?

The deed
is never a good deed
unless the motivation is right and true.
When we are driven by
anger, hatred, malice, or contempt,
we can never love another.
When we are motivated by
lust, greed, envy, or jealousy,
we can never love another.
When we are slaves to
self-seeking, deceit, or false attitudes,
we can never love another.

How dangerous the teacher
who points out that
sin is the basic motivation in everything

I think, do, and say.
No one without sin.
No one able not to sin,
when all the time I thought
there were no serious sins in my life.

What to do with such a teacher?
Reject him.
Ridicule him.
Crucify him.
Such a teacher cannot be from God.
I know God.
I love God.
I serve him.
A teacher who makes me feel guilty,
when there is no reason for guilt,
cannot be from God.

The Fulfillment

Jesus said,
"I have not come to abolish the law
and the prophets,
but to fulfill them."
He did not abolish the commandments.
He placed them in a true, realistic perspective.
Not the deed but the motive.
Not the act, but the desire and intention
of our heart determines
whether or not our deeds are true
and acceptable to God.

Love!
Total, unconditional love
for every other,
whether husband or wife,
friend or foe,
is to characterize our attitude and our relationship
in our home,
our community,

at our place of work,
in the business world,
and in our gender and racial attitudes and relationships.

It is to be and to do
what Carol Stuart's parents did in Boston,
when Carol was killed by her husband.
Her premature baby dead.
Charles wrongly identified a black man
from Mission Hill
as the killer.
Rage and fury in the Afro-American community.
Carol's parents
established a foundation for scholarships
for blacks from Mission Hill.
This is fulfilling Jesus' command to love
unconditionally.

Jesus did not come
to destroy the law of God.
He came to lift it above our will and our purpose;
above pettiness,
partiality, and prejudice
to a new and exalted level of purpose and meaning
for the people of God.

The Apostle Paul,
with rare insight into the purpose and meaning
of Jesus' teaching,
wrote,
"You are no longer under the law.
You are free from its requirement."
He compares our new situation
to a woman,
widowed by the death of her husband,
"You are no longer bound by the law of marriage.
You are free
to marry another."

The Dot and the Iota

The man and the woman in Christ
have been set free
from slavish obedience to a commandment.
No longer do we need to be told
by the commandment,
"You shall not kill.
You shall not commit adultery.
You shall not swear falsely.
You shall love your neighbor
as you love yourself."

The will of God
reaches new levels of expression
when we are in the Spirit.
The Spirit is
God's power given to every baptized believer,
empowering us to love,
to be honest in word and intention,
to be modest and chaste in conduct,
to love even our enemy
who despises, ridicules,
or even takes our life.

"Not an iota, not a dot
will pass from the law,"
Jesus said.
Even the small vowel pointings,
even the smallest letter will stand.
This is the eternal and immutable will of God.
God does not excuse our failures.
He forgives.

He forgives those who earnestly seek him,
who seriously seek to make amends
for wrongs done;
to heal the wounds
and to right the wrongs we have done.

The deadly attitudes of
malice, envy, jealousy, bitterness,

pride and selfishness,
prejudice and self-righteousness
we carry through life,
are to be laid at the feet of Jesus.
We are free,
for we are in Christ and Christ is in us.

The Family of God

God's purpose,
according to the teaching and example of Jesus, is
to mold us and all people
of every race and class and culture
into one family:
the family of God.

We are the new,
the one family of God,
loving and caring
for every other member of our family
on Planet Earth.
We are to radiate love and joy,
peace and good will
to a world of people broken and fragmented
by godlessness,
hate, bitterness, prejudice,
greed, lust, falseness,
and overbearing egotism.

We are love personified,
not embalmed in commandments,
but alive in the Spirit of him who said,
"Not a dot, not an iota,
shall fall from the law."
Love living and active in the lives
of my people,
washed and cleansed
by the waters of baptism
and nourished daily upon word and sacrament.

The Dot and the Iota

"Let the Spirit of Christ
dwell in you richly,"
said the Apostle.
Be open to God,
responsive to his will.
Tread in the footsteps of our Lord
who walked the paths of life
in tune with God's will and purpose.
Then, and then only,
are God's dots and iotas
fulfilled in you.

15

Blessings and Woes

The Sixth Sunday after the Epiphany

Luke 6.20–26

Then he looked up at his disciples and said,
"Blessed are you who are poor,
for yours is the kingdom of God.
"Blessed are you who are hungry now,
for you will be filled.
"Blessed are you who weep now,
for you will rejoice.
"Blessed are you when people hate you, and when they
exclude and revile you, on account of the Son
of man. Rejoice in that day and leap for joy,
for surely your reward is great in heaven; for
that is what their ancestors did to the prophets.
"Woe you who are rich,
for you have received your consolation.
"Woe to you who are full now,
for you will be hungry.
"Woe to you who are laughing now,
for you will mourn and weep.
"Woe to you when all speak well of you,
for that is what their ancestors did
to the false prophets."

Luther Memorial Church
Burbank, California

Blessings and Woes

Jesus often spoke in radical terms—
words that clash
with our customary and popular ways
of thinking.
The blessings and the woes
are examples of his radical teaching.

How beautifully they sound in our hearing.
"Blessed are you poor.
Blessed are you who hunger.
Blessed are you who weep.
Blessed are you who are hated for my sake."
We need to probe the very depths of these sayings
for the meaning and intention of Jesus.
They are so contrary to our ways of thinking.

There is a depth to these sayings
that we often fail to understand.
We hear the "Blesseds,"
but fail to perceive the deep undertones.

The "Blesseds" are attacks
upon our popular ways of thinking;
ways of thinking that give priority
to a material, not a spiritual,
understanding of life.

Let us consider the "Blesseds"
from a spiritual point of view
to learn what was the intention of Jesus.
Only in this way
can our lives, our ways of thought,
and our deeds
be shaped and molded
by the word of God.

Blessed are You Poor

Jesus said,
"Blessed are you poor."
How can this be true,
since poverty is a sign of "Woe."
A sign of God's disfavor.
We are not poor,
but there are millions and even billions
in our world who suffer grinding poverty.
We may not be wealthy,
but we live above the level of poverty and want.

Poverty is a condition in life,
we say.
the result of a lack of the discipline
of hard work and frugality.
People are poor because they do not apply themselves
to the rigor of providing for their needs.
The poor could do it on their own,
if they would make the effort.

We have an innate feeling of contempt
for those who are dependent
because they will not provide for themselves.
If they had an ounce of gumption
they would not be poor.
There is a way to avoid poverty.
We could do this ourselves,
if we only made the effort.

Jesus said,
"Blessed are you poor."
He reversed the common view
that to be rich is a sign of God's favor
and poverty a sign of his disfavor.
We have the idea that the thinking and rules
of this world
apply to God as well.

Blessings and Woes

We create an image of God in our image.
God created all of us to be rich.
Some are not rich because they do not try hard enough.
They are content to live on a public dole.
We forget that many are born into slavery;
slavery to their heritage.
Born into a history of poverty
from the beginnings of the human race.
Many are born with handicaps;
the lack of the mental and physical gifts
necessary to provide for the basic needs in life.

Many lack the privilege of opportunity
to improve their situation in life.
There are those who have lifted themselves
by their bootstraps
from poverty to wealth,
but there has been that fortuitous event
that has opened the door
to success in life.

I was such a one.
Son of a poor dirt farmer according to human standards.
Destined to be a tenant farmer,
or a day laborer.
A high school graduate in the depths of the depression.
A suggestion by a friend five years later,
"Go to college.
Others have worked their way through."
The door opened
and I entered in,
not entirely by my own efforts, however.
There was encouragement,
unusual, gracious, and unexpected financial support
that contributed to my opportunity.
By the grace of God and by financial help
even from strangers,
I received the highest degree
from one of the premier educational institutions
of our land.

Bread? or Crumbs?

Not many in the poverty class
have had such a "Blessed" in life.
Jesus' word,
"Blessed are the poor,"
is a radical departure from the contemporary view
that poverty is always the result
of our poor judgment,
our lack of discipline
our sloth,
our failure to plan for our future.

Successful people are often overly proud
of their success.
Some are deserving of honor,
but many inherited the possibility for success,
and were able by wealth and the right connections
to continue a family tradition.

Birth into the right family;
or the possession of material wealth,
do not earn a "Blessed,"
according to Jesus.
He said to a rich young man,
"How difficult it is for a rich person
to enter the kingdom of God."
He added,
"Go, sell what you possess,
and give to the poor,
and you will have treasure in heaven;
and come, follow me."

Wealth is even a hindrance
to a "Blessed."
Jesus also said,
"Woe to you who are rich."
God's measure for success is never
material wealth.
Our priorities are wrong
whenever riches and security

Blessings and Woes

are our goal in life,
and God plays a secondary role in our affections.

We may reside in a stately mansion.
We may be wealthy in land,
stocks and bonds
The danger is,
as Jesus pointed out again and again,
that we become slaves
to that which is not God.
We cannot buy into heaven,
as we can into many an exclusive club.

"Blessed are you poor,"
said Jesus,
Blessed are you when you rely upon God
for life, health,
and salvation.
"Blessed are you,"
who have been captured by the mind and spirit
of Christ.

Now pride and self-righteousness
are forever overthrown.
No longer do they rule
in the great and critical decisions
that reveal our true character
and our true relationship
to God
and to one another.

Blessed Are You Hungry

Jesus said,
"Blessed are you hungry."
Have you and I known deep and painful hunger?
Hunger to the point of death?
Our problem is not hunger.
Our problem is we are too full;
Addicted to a way of life

that seeks satisfaction in abundance.
We are full of substitutes and imitations for the real thing.

Years ago a shaving company,
Burma Shave,
had a series of roadside signs along the highways.
One in particular is appropriate in this context.
"Substitutes and imitations.
Send them to your wife's relations.
Burma Shave."
We have become a people
of substitutes and imitations for the real thing.

This is what Jesus is talking about.
There is a spiritual condition in life
that majors in the minors,
in the adiaphora,
the non-essentials.
Let us look at the world around us.
Big is better.
Let us build bigger barns.
Let us drive bigger cars.
Let us put more fast food upon the table.

Our mania for things is the subject of
Jesus' teaching.
"Woe to you who are full now."
We are full.
Full of cheap religion.
Satisfied with a do-it-ourselves religion.
Pleased with a god of our own making.
Created in our own image.

Jesus was talking about the idolatry,
the false gods,
that commanded the allegiance of God's chosen people.
Worship in the temple had become
worship of the temple.
Love for neighbor had become
a discrimination against anyone

of a different race or culture.
They said of Jesus,
"Can any good thing come out of Galilee?"
Impossible!
Good things could only come out of Judea.
Rules for the practice of religion made it impossible
for humble people like shepherds
to qualify for rightness with God.
Their calling in life
out in the fields with their flocks,
made it impossible for them to fulfill
the strict conditions of religion—
diet, worship, sacrifices,
the keeping of feast days.

Luke is the gospel writer who emphasizes
in a singular way
the teaching of Jesus
set forth in this beatitude and woe.
"Blessed are you poor."
"Woe to you who are rich."

To whom do the angels appear
at the birth of the Christ child?
Not to the priests, the Sadducees,
who presided over the religion of the state.
Not to the pious, self-righteous Pharisees,
who could thank God that they were not as other men.
Not to the rich and well-born
in their comfortable quarters,
full of all the good things in life.
But to lowly shepherds
out in the field tending their sheep at night.
Shepherds even despised by all of the above
because of their vocation.
Shepherds!
who provided lambs for the necessary sacrifices.

So it is whenever our priorities
have replaced the priorities of God.

Bread? or Crumbs?

Jesus reverses our understanding of God
and of God's requirement of us.
Not the "full" people,
but the "hungry" people
have the mark of approval of God
upon their foreheads.

Down with the gods of plenty.
Down with the gods of emotion.
Down with the gods of greed
and lust for power.
Up with the God of the humble.
Up with the God of the disenfranchised,
the poor,
despised because of their lowly status in life.

What a contrast to our image of God.
The empty will be filled,
and the filled will be turned empty away.
Can this be true?
Sad to say it is true.
We who are full have no special status with God.
The poor are his favorites.
The poor know their lack
and their utter dependence upon God.

Blessed are You Weepers

Jesus said,
"Blessed are you who weep.
You shall laugh and sing for joy."
What a wonderful gift is laughter.
How pleasing
the sound of laughter to the ear.
How sad, how pitiful
the sounds of grief—sobs and tears.

There is gloom and doom in our lives.
Often it is sorrow
because we are denied the trinkets and toys

that make us feel good.
Often it is frustration
because we fail to reach the goals
and successes we crave.
Often it is the agony we suffer inside
when a dear one is taken from us by death,
and we remember what could and should have been
if we had only been more loving,
more patient, more giving of ourselves.
Now it is too late.

What a tragedy
that we have corrupted the gift of laughter
by cheap and maudlin entertainers
who lampoon and ridicule
fellow humans.
Entertainers who joke about sacred things—
religion, marriage, truth,
chastity and integrity.

Laughter is a wonderful gift from God.
True joy springs eternal
from the spirit of the one
who knows the eternal presence of God
in the little things of everyday life.
Jesus said,
"Blessed are you weepers."

Blessed are you
who are sad and mournful
about the state and condition of the human spirit.
Sad about the shallowness
of the ideals and values of people everywhere.
Sad about the fraud, the deception,
the duplicity, the dishonesty,
the lack of character
that sweeps away like a mighty tide
the most precious gifts of all—
faith, hope, and love.
Gifts God has generously shared with us
in our Lord Jesus

Above all, Jesus makes known
that sad and tragic events in our life
are not marks of God's disfavor.
The Apostle Paul
enumerates long lists of the griefs
that troubled him daily.
In the midst of the most trying times in his life
he wrote,
"Rejoice in the Lord always.
Again I will say rejoice."

How comforting to know that in the time
of our deepest grief,
a grief about our own spiritual lack,
our failures and shortcomings,
our Lord can say,
"Blessed are you who weep now,
for you shall laugh."

How sad to hear his word,
"Woe to you who are laughing now,
for you will mourn and weep."
How sad that the multitudes take pleasure
in the obscene,
in the gaudy and profane;
that our sense of all that is ennobling and uplifting
to the human spirit
has been cheapened and degraded
by our frenzied music,
the violence portrayed in literature and drama,
our mania for sports
that has corrupted our educational system.

In the midst of such travesties in our times,
we hear words of hope and encouragement.
Our future will be brighter and better.
God is still the Lord of heaven and earth.
He says to us emphatically,
"Blessed are you who weep now,
for you shall laugh."

Blessings and Woes

Blessed Are You Who Are Hated

Jesus said,
"Blessed are you who are hated,
excluded, reviled, and defamed now."
What a strange saying.
We yearn to be loved and wanted,
to be received as equals,
to be treated with respect and dignity.

The way of the world is quite different
from the ways of God.
We draw lines in the sand.
Circles that include all those who are acceptable
in our eyes.
Outside of that circle are all those who suffer
gender bias,
racial prejudice,
religious persecution,
all those who are called "liberal" in a pejorative sense.
They are the poor, the maimed,
the lame, the lepers
in Jesus time who were excluded from society,
set adrift in a world
marred by hatred and discrimination.

Times have not changed.
We all have our straw people we beat upon
because they do not measure up
to our standard
of what a human should be.
It makes us feel superior and righteous
to know
that there are so many who fall beneath
our levels of excellence—
Standards set by our good opinion of ourselves.

So we too exclude, revile, defame
and hate
those who are created by the God

Bread? or Crumbs?

who created us.
Who created them in his image,
just as we are created in his image.

Let it not be so,
said Jesus
How wonderful to be loved and accepted.
To be treated as equals
with compassion and kindness.
But it is not so.
How hateful we can be to others;
even to the ones we love.

How that perverse streak in us
manifests itself
as the Apostle Paul describes,
"The good that I would do,
I do not do;
the evil that I would not do,
I do.
Wretched man that I am.
Who will deliver me from this body of death?"

There is another dimension
to the saying of Jesus.
We exclude, revile, defame, and hate
"on account of the Son of man."
There is religious persecution in our time.
There has been religious persecution
from the beginning of time.
Egyptians in the time of Joseph
could not eat with Hebrews.
"That was an abomination to them."
The people of God created their own image of God
when they had their god say to them,
"Kill the Canaanites."
Were not the Canaanites God's creation too?

So it has been down through the ages.
Christians killing Muslims

and Muslims killing Christians.
The Crusades,
a horrible chapter in our history.
More Christians killed by one another in the Crusades
than Muslims.
The terrible religious wars
of Christians against Christians—
Protestants against Catholics
and Catholics against Protestants.
The inquisition.
A Joan of Arc burned at the stake,
and witches in Massachusetts.

When will it all end?
Is our generation different from earlier generations?
There are martyrs for the faith today.
Hundreds and even thousands.
Can it be true,
"Blessed are you the hated ones;
Rejoice and leap for joy,
for your reward will be great?"
This is the eternal promise of God.

There is a kind of undercurrent
of hatred latent in our psyche too.
We too suppress others from voicing the truth
because it is contrary to
our ways of thinking and belief.
How often we are deterred
from making our convictions known
because of our fear
of a negative reaction from family or friends.
Afraid to defend the truth
for fear we will offend the sensitivities of those
who really have no genuine sensitivity
for any other than themselves.

How pleased we are
when others speak well of us.
Our ego satiated and nourished by praise.

How gifted we are at self praise.
Mother said to me on a number of occasions,
"Self praise stinks."

How can we accept this word from Jesus?
"Blessed are you who are hated.
Woe to you when all speak well of you."
It is most difficult,
for it is so different from our self esteem,
our pride and vanity.
It is true nevertheless,
for our God has spoken,
"My ways are not your ways,
and your ways are not my ways."

The Summary

How strange these words of Jesus.
How contrary to all the norms
that we live by in real life.
How true nevertheless in the real world
of the kingdom of God.

"Blessed are the poor.
Woe to you who are rich.
Blessed are the hungry.
Woe to you who are full.
Blessed are the weepers.
Woe to you who laugh."
God's ways are not our ways.

Our sinful nature even rebels against
the voice of God
who reverses our concept
of our own self-importance,
and of our demeaning of others
who threaten
our sense of superiority.

Blessings and Woes

God's love would set us free
from the bondage,
this baggage that would drag us down
to the pit.
Truth hurts,
but it is the only medicine
that heals us of our pride and self-righteousness.
How often Jesus cried out
against these human traits
that are so common to all of us.

How often we major in the negatives,
in the minors.
Finding the speck of dust in the eye of another,
when the log is in our own eye.

We are rich only when the Spirit of Christ
dwells in us richly.
We are full only when the grace of God
abides in us daily.
We are joyful only when the peace of God
radiates in and through us
in every situation in life.
We are blessed
when we are persecuted, reviled, defamed
for our faith in the Christ.

This is God's promise
to you and to me today.
A promise duly made and sealed
with the blood of his beloved Son,
Jesus Christ, our Lord.
Amen.
Praise the Lord.
Hallelujah.

16

The Sun and the Rain

The Seventh Sunday after the Epiphany

Matthew 5.38–48

"You have heard that it was said, 'An eye for an eye and a tooth for a tooth.' I say to you, Do not resist an evildoer. If anyone strikes you on the right cheek, turn the other also; and if anyone wants to sue you and take your coat, give your cloak as well; if anyone forces you to go one mile, go also the second mile. Give to every one who begs from you, and do not refuse anyone who wants to borrow from you.

"You have heard that it was said, 'You shall love your neighbor, and hate your enemy.' I say to you, Love your enemies, and pray for those who persecute you, so that you may be children of your Father in heaven; for he makes his sun rise on the evil and on the good, and sends rain on the righteous and on the unrighteous. If you love those who love you, what reward do you have? Do not even tax collectors do the same? If you greet only your brothers and sisters, what more are you doing than others? Do not even Gentiles do the same? Be perfect, therefore, as your heavenly Father is perfect."

Our Savior's Lutheran Church
Oxnard, California

The Sun and the Rain

The sun
and the rain!
The gifts of God to his creation.
The sun
rises early in the morning
to warm the earth,
to provide energy
for all the earth's functions,
and to sustain life for all plants and animals.
The rain,
falling gently upon the earth,
shares the necessary moisture to sustain the life
of all plants and animals too.

The sun
and the rain!
Provide all that is necessary
to generate and sustain life.
We praise God
for the gifts of sun and rain
without which we could not be.

Illustrations of God's Care

Jesus said,
"God makes his sun rise
on the evil and on the good,
and sends rain
on the righteous and the unrighteous."
Jesus paints a picture
of the nature of our heavenly Father.
God is love.
He does not withhold sun and rain
from any one of us,
ungrateful and wicked though we may be.
God the Lord is gracious!
His mercy is forever!

Bread? or Crumbs?

How different from our ways.
We convert evil into good
by threat of punishment
or promise of reward.
We promote good behavior with the carrot,
and restrain bad behavior
by threat of the stick.
This is not the way of your heavenly Father,
said Jesus.

God is our model for conduct.
We are created in the image of God,
shaped and molded out of rude clay
to be like him
in our rule and dominion over the earth.
God is our model
for the way we are to live in community
with one another.

How may we describe this picture of God
Jesus draws with his pen?
God is true.
God is impartial,
God is loving and merciful to all,
even the hostile,
the undeserving,
the profane,
to those who have no room for God
in heart or home.

The sun,
a mighty star in the heavens,
never, never singles out a good person
for special favor,
or withholds its life-giving rays
from the wicked.
The sun
sheds its life sustaining rays
upon all without distinction.

The Sun and the Rain

The rain
bathes the earth
with life-giving, life-sustaining moisture,
falling upon all of God's creatures,
never singling out a few
for special favor,
nor withholding its bounty
from the many.

What would life be on earth
without such impartiality and equity?
God the Lord is gracious.
The sun and the rain are to us
what they are
because he is impartial.
He is forever true to his nature.
He loves all that he has made.

We are created and called to be examples
of God's graciousness and love
on Planet Earth.
This is the heart of the message of the gospel.
Jesus said,
"You and I are to be perfect,
as perfect as God is perfect."
Goodness, fairness,
equity, and love
are to be as natural for us
in our relationships with one another
as they are to God.

We are called by our Lord
to know and understand
that goodness is only goodness
when goodness is for goodness sake.
We are to be good
as God is good,
loving, kind, true,
faithful in every relationship
to the good earth
and to all who inhabit the good earth.

Bread? or Crumbs?

God acts according to his nature.
God is good all the time,
because that is the way he is at heart.
There is no evil, malice,
or vindictiveness in God.

We are to be fashioned in his image
in all that we are
and all that we do in our thoughts,
words, and deeds.
We are to be the mirrors of God
in daily life.
We are to show this mirror of God
to one another:
to our family, our neighbor,
and to the stranger far and near.

Our problem:
We show quite a different image,
an image shaped and molded by our own
selfish desires.
An image mirroring our inner desires—
lust, greed, hate,
jealousy, envy,
selfishness, and godlessness.

If we had the power
to control the rays of the sun
and the raindrops that fall,
would they shine and fall equally on all?
Or would the sun shine
and the rain fall
only upon a select few
whom we choose to control and use
for our own enrichment and pleasure?

This is the question of the day
that challenges us
as Jesus speaks from the heart
to our heart, our mind, and spirit.

The Eye and the Tooth

In days of old,
when man first appeared upon the earth,
it was the custom
to kill and destroy an enemy or an offender.
Equity, fairness,
a sense of morality were lacking.
Survival of the fittest
was the rule governing human conduct
and relationships.

There were the beginnings
of a sense of equity and fairness
for one's own,
but never for the stranger;
for those outside the circle drawn in the sand
to distinguish
my people from your people.

Alas!
Even those within the charmed circle
were victims
of the greed, the lust,
and the hunger for power
of those at the head of the pecking order
whenever they stood in the way
of the selfish, ambitious goals
of the strong and powerful.

Abel,
slain by his brother, Cain,
out of jealousy and envy
because Cain thought God favored Abel.
After all,
Cain reasoned,
"I am the elder.
I deserve better,
for I should take precedence over my brother."

Bread? or Crumbs?

After generations of time,
a higher level of understanding developed,
"An eye for an eye and a tooth for a tooth."
Insult and injury
were to be punished,
but only in the measure of the damage inflicted
by the wrongdoer.
A punishment beyond the damage done
deserved a counter retaliation.

How was it possible to inflict damage
upon a tooth
without injuring another tooth?
The code of conduct still at a level
that created more problems
than it resolved.

A beginning had been made
to weigh in the scales of justice
a fair response
and retaliation for an injustice.
But the proof of the taste is in the pudding.
How difficult to restrain
the impulse for vengeance,
for revenge,
from the response to wrongdoing,
since the heart of man
was still enslaved
to all the passions of bitterness,
hatred, malice,
and the inner desire to do more than get even.

Jesus came from God
to implant within us a new sense of morality,
a new sense of right conduct.
"Do not resist evil.
Turn the other cheek.
Give your cloak as well.
Go the second mile."
What a beautiful mirror of what we are to be
in our relationships with one another.

What a difficult way to follow.
Impossible for any one of us.
Consider our conduct
when we are offended,
we who live under the mantle of Christ.
Do we turn the other cheek?
Or go the second mile?
Family members at war with one another
over trivialities.

Two brothers in North Carolina
in a community where I resided,
at war with one another over a property line.
The two met at the scene of the dispute,
the one represented by an attorney.
The one shot the brother and his attorney
over a few feet of land
that probably had little or no value to either.

An isolated incident?
We all have been touched at one time or another
by the same kind of feuding.
A dispute over a few dishes
or a chair
at the time of the dividing up of the inheritance.
Have we ever turned the other cheek?
Or gone the second mile?

How often we choose
to live by the ancient law:
"An eye for an eye and a tooth for a tooth,"
rather than by the Spirit of him
who said,
"Love your neighbor."

Who even took the Spirit of love and forgiveness
to new and higher levels,
when he said,
"Love your enemy."

Bread? or Crumbs?

His teaching is a new teaching
in the history of humankind.

Our attitude towards one another,
towards our neighbor,
the stranger, to people everywhere,
even to the far reaches of the earth,
are to be conditioned
by the love of God in us.
The sun rises on the evil and on the good;
the rain falls on the righteous and the unrighteous.

The role model
for our attitudes and our conduct
is none other than
Jesus of Nazareth.
Those who knew him most intimately wrote,
"He committed no sin.
No guile was found on his lips.
When he was reviled,
he did not revile in return.
When he suffered, he did not threaten."
He lived
by his own teaching even to death.

Our Model for Life

Jesus is our model.
We are to pattern our life and conduct
after his example.
His love, his kindness,
his benevolence and forgiveness,
are to be grafted upon our hearts.

Vengeance,
an eye for an eye or a tooth for a tooth,
can never mend broken relationships
or put the broken pieces together again.
Like humpty-dumpty,
they are forever shattered.

The Sun and the Rain

An eye for an eye and a tooth for a tooth
are always the breeding ground
for renewed warfare,
for more deadly attacks upon one another.

How can a broken relationship be renewed,
if you put out my eye
and I strike yours in return?
What thoughts and feelings grip our hearts
as we look upon
the damaged eye of the other?

Never can there be a family under God
until our motives
for revenge and retaliation
are rooted from our minds and hearts.
Only the love of God
planted deeply within us can transform us
into the people of God who
"Love the enemy,"
as God loves all that he has made,
even the worst of sinners.

Jesus accepted death,
a cruel, inhumane, wrongful death,
quietly, serenely,
rather than permit a spirit of revenge,
or vindictiveness,
mar the peace of his heart and mind.

We are imperfect and sinful.
We most often fall short of the model
God has given
by which we are to fashion our life style.
This may be excusable
when done in ignorance,
but never
when we have heard the teachings
of the one who said,
"Forgive,
and it will be forgiven you."

Bread? or Crumbs?

Those who know not the Christ
may commit crimes of inhumanity,
of meanness and cruelty,
of revenge and even murder.
Never, never are such attitudes
leading to such awful deeds
to find lodging in our hearts.
We bear the mark of the cross of Christ
upon our brow.
His Spirit has been planted in the deepest levels
of our self.
We have died with Christ;
we have come alive in him in our baptism.

Malice and bitterness,
anger and hatred,
jealousy and ill will
are to be forever renounced by all of us
who are called by the name of Christ.

Love, truth,
goodness, honesty, integrity,
fairness and equity
are to prevail in our world
created by the Lord God.
We who have died in Christ
and who are alive in him
are to carry these gifts into the world,
a world broken and fragmented
by human greed and selfishness.

Our Lord Jesus
took giant steps on the road
to the fulfillment of God's purpose
by his example
of love and forgiveness to all.
We who are called by his name
are to forge new pathways and take giant steps
in love and forgiveness

for one another
and especially for our enemy.

Love one another.
Forgive, if any one has wronged you.
Do good to those who abuse you.
Turn the other cheek.
Give to the one who sues your cloak also.
Go the second mile.
Give to the one who begs from you.
Love your enemy.
Pray for the persecutor.
Be perfect as your heavenly Father is perfect.

God is like that.
We are the creation of God,
fashioned in his image.
Redeemed from the deadly pestilence
of malice and bitterness,
vengeance and hatred.
We are to show the face of God
wherever we are
and in whatever situation is ours in life.

We are in the time period
when we celebrate the birthday
of one our great presidents,
Abraham Lincoln.
We are called to emulate with sincerity
the face he showed towards the enemy
in the crucible of a terrible war,
when he said,
"With malice towards none,
and with charity for all."
This thought could only have issued
from the heart of God.

We celebrate the victory of Jesus
over the powers of retaliation and revenge
when we respond to slander, gossip,

Bread? or Crumbs?

or wrongful accusation
like the parents of Carol Stuart of Boston.
They established a scholarship
in the name of their daughter
for needy Afro-American children
from Mission Hill,
because one of their community was wrongfully accused
of the murder of their daughter.

Jesus' invitation to us
is a clarion call,
"Go forth into the world in my name."
Plant the ideal of love and forgiveness
in your family relations,
in your community
in your church,
at your place of work,
in your business,
and in whatever situation you find yourself in life.

Forgive when wronged,
Turn the other cheek.
Go the second mile.
Love your enemy.
What an order for our walk through life.
This we can do only with the help of God.

These are marching orders for the people of God.
Jesus said,
"I appoint you; I anoint you,"
to be Christ to your neighbor,
to the stranger,
to the wrongdoer,
to your enemy.

Let love rise with the morning sun
and shine throughout the day
upon the evil and upon the good.
Let your compassion and forgiveness
flow like a mighty stream

The Sun and the Rain

upon the righteous and the unrighteous.
You are the called and chosen.
Called and chosen to be my missionaries
in the world.

God the Lord is gracious!
His mercy endures forever.

17

Three Booths, a Cloud, and a Voice

The Day of the Transfiguration of Our Lord

Matthew 17.1–9

Six days later Jesus took with him, Peter and James and his brother John and led them up a high mountain, by themselves. He was transfigured before them, and his face shone like the sun, and his clothes became dazzling white. Suddenly there appeared to them Moses and Elijah, talking with him. Then Peter said to Jesus, "Lord, it is good for us to be here; if you wish, I will make three booths here; one for you, one for Moses, and one for Elijah." While he was still speaking, suddenly a bright cloud overshadowed them, and from the cloud a voice said, "This is my Son, the Beloved; with him I am well pleased; listen to him!" When his disciples heard this, they fell to the ground and were overcome by fear. But Jesus came and touched them, saying, "Get up, and do not be afraid." And when they looked up, they saw no one but Jesus only.

St. Andrews Lutheran Church
Andrews, North Carolina

Three Booths, a Cloud, and a Voice

Mountain climbing
takes skill and stamina.
We are surrounded by mountains,
but they are small
compared to other mountain peaks
on Planet Earth—
the Himalayas,
the Alps,
the Andes,
the Rockies,
our Mount Whitney and Mount McKinley.

Mountain peaks,
piercing the heavens
twenty thousand feet or more.
Only a few hardy climbers
can scale such heights.
It is dangerous.
Many have lost their lives
in the attempt.

Our mountain peaks
are more our style.
They are not killers,
although they can be dangerous.
If we have scaled a mountain peak,
we know how rewarding it is
to view
the panoramic sight from a great height.

A mountain peak is a unique spot
to relax
and contemplate the serious questions of life
with the world at our feet.

Three Booths

One day Jesus climbed
such a peak in Galilee

Bread? or Crumbs?

with Peter, James, and John.
The experience was unforgettable.
Jesus was transfigured before them.
He glowed
with a heavenly radiance.

When I was a youth,
I attended my first Bible Camp
on the shores of a beautiful Minnesota lake.
Four of us camped in a pasture
in pup tents.
We could not afford the cabin rates.
We chopped wood for our camp fire,
a fire for preparing our meals.

An old stump was fuel
for our fire.
One evening there was a heavy rainfall.
When we returned to our camp
after the evening Bible study,
the ground was aglow
with a brilliant luminescent light.
The old stump had decomposed
into what is called phosphorescent wood.
What a beautiful sight!

After such an experience,
I can imagine in my mind's eye
the beauty of Jesus,
radiantly aglow
in all the brilliance and glory of God.

Peter was so overwhelmed and thrilled
by the glory of Jesus,
aglow in all the radiance of God,
that he wanted to remain there forever.
"Let us build three booths here;
three dwelling places,"
he said.
Let us make this our dwelling place;

this peaceful, quiet place
away from the madding crowd.

Let us spend our days here.
Why return to the valley,
to the hustle and bustle of life?
"What a noble sentiment,"
we say,
"to spend the rest of our earthly days
in peace and bliss
with Jesus only."

Here we may peacefully contemplate
the glory of God
and all the glory of the earth,
God's lovely creation.
Here we can be free,
undisturbed by the cares and anxieties of life.

What a delightful and inviting prospect—
to live in peaceful bliss,
untroubled by the cares and anxieties
of life in the midst
of a chaotic world.
How pleasant to contemplate
a withdrawal from the world
to a place where we can be alone with our God.
Even the Word of God
seems to suggest such a goal in life,
for the Word says,
"Love not the world;
nor the things that are of this world."

When I was a youth,
a member of the Four-H Club,
we sang a song at our get-togethers,
"We'll build a little nest,
somewhere in the West,
and let the rest of the world go by."

Bread? or Crumbs?

The world is filled with trouble and sorrow,
a dangerous place.
Life is sometimes difficult and demanding.
There is no peaceful time
or place
to bask in the glory and beauty of God
and of his creation.
Where is there a quiet place
to be alone
for meditation and for peaceful bliss?

What a temptation!
Burdened and overwhelmed
by the demands of daily life,
how wonderful
to find that quiet place
where we can be free from responsibilities
and obligations
that weigh so heavily upon us.

What better place to realize our dream
than upon a mountain top,
or a secluded glen
away from the cares and troubles of life.

Let us carry with us to our quiet place
the opportunity to contemplate
unendingly the blessings of our religion.
Let us cherish our faith,
unchallenged by the worldly temptations and cares.
Let us be free from temptations
to grieve our Lord
by sinning, by living below
the levels of his expectations for us.

Let us, with Peter, plan
to build a quiet place for Jesus,
for Moses and Elijah,
for all the saints whom we adore.
Let us sit at their feet
and drink deeply of the wells of inspiration.

Three Booths, a Cloud, and a Voice

All we need for the holy life is here—
the law,
the prophetic word,
the comforting word of our Savior.
Where could we practice our faith
more securely,
more appropriately,
than upon a mountain top,
away from all that would disturb our tranquillity?
Is there anything more disturbing
to true religion
than the noise of people,
who break into our peaceful thoughts?
People who cause resentment,
even anger,
because we want to be alone in meditation and prayer?

Once upon a time,
but not too long ago,
a man and his wife visited our worship
at St. Paul's Lutheran
in Ansonia, Connecticut.
It was the Sunday
I baptized my beautiful little daughter Susan.
They never returned to worship.
They were unchurched Lutherans.
They never returned
because the presence of little children disturbed them.
Worship was to be a quiet place;
not a place for children.

So it is for some.
For those truly religious spirits
who believe
the meaning and purpose of life
is to contemplate
the glory,
the beauty,
the holiness of God

in quietness and peace
without disturbance even from God's little children.
Did not Jesus say,
"Let the little ones come to me?"

The Cloud

But alas!
God does not permit such choices.
Just when we have experienced
the rich and rewarding
mountain top experience;
Just when we think
we have attained the place
for the perfect life in Christ,
there is an intrusion from above.
There is a cloud!
Perhaps a bright and shining cloud,
but a cloud
that casts a huge shadow nevertheless.

It is the ever present God
breaking into our religiousness,
into our pious thoughts,
pointing to the true meaning
of our encounter with the Christ.

God in his glory and majesty
outshines the sun.
How dangerous to look directly at the shining sun.
How we are blinded
by its brilliant rays.
Only a momentary glance
and our eye must return to earth.

In like manner
we cannot remain upon the mountain top.
The imperatives of life
are in the valley below.
Here we rub elbows with one another,

with our neighbor.
Here we find our true calling in life—
to love and serve one another.

There is a time,
a necessary time,
to go apart from the world
and from our neighbor
to that quiet place,
to a mountain top for renewal,
to recharge the batteries of our inner self.
To remain there, however, is not possible.

The genuine spiritual life
is not lived in solitude.
It is not here that we come to know the God
of our salvation,
our Creator, our Redeemer,
the Spirit who moves and inspires us
to share the grace of God
with our neighbor
and throughout the world.

No!
It is in our neighbor we see God;
in the sick and needy,
in the naked and hungry,
in the imprisoned
and in those afflicted by
the demons of addiction and passion.

We see God,
we are renewed and strengthened
for our calling
in the quiet place,
amidst the quiet trees
and the green, listening sod.
We come here for renewal,
for refueling,
to fulfill our calling in the valley below.

Bread? or Crumbs?

We see God not only
in the beauty and majesty
of the heavenly blue above,
decorated
in billows of white,
untainted by the smog and dirt
from man's capacity to pollute God's wonderful creation.

We see him not only
out of sight of our neighbor,
in the quiet place where we are undisturbed
by the cares and troubles
that assail us and the people around us.
Wherever our retreat from life in the world
becomes the idyllic place
for genuine spiritual life,
there appears the cloud
shattering our dream.
The bright and shining cloud,
menacing nevertheless,
recalling us to the true realities
of God's purpose for us
when he made us his own in baptism.

When we are alive in the Spirit of God,
we see the cloud.
We know the ever present God is calling us
to our place of service
in the world.

The Voice

The cloud is nothing in itself
without the voice,
bright and shining though it may be.
Who can read God's message
in a cloud?
What a gorgeous reflection it is
high in the sky,

Three Booths, a Cloud, and a Voice

a reflection of the Creator God
who has made all things in his love.
There they are,
roll upon roll of beautiful white billows,
sometimes silhouetting
a face or a figure familiar to us
from our earth-bound pose.
Or again,
a dark and menacing figure,
foreshadowing the fearful storm
with powerful winds,
mighty peals of thunder,
and bright shafts of lightning
searing the sky.

The cloud has a voice;
mighty peals of thunder,
crying out in fearful language,
demonstrating the mighty power
of him who made it.
The voice,
speaking to Peter, James, and John
on the mountain top was not like that.

That cloud
had a voice of its own—
The voice of the one who had made it,
the voice of God himself.
God speaking
from the mountain top,
from the quiet place,
saying,
"Go down into the valley.
Go, where I would have you be,
working for me in the valley of life."

Go where the people are.
My people crying out in the darkness
for light and life.
Go, announce to them

Bread? or Crumbs?

the glorious glad tidings,
"This Jesus is my beloved Son.
I send him to you for your salvation.
I send him to you that you may find that quiet place
wherever you are,
even in the midst of a loud and frantic world.
I send him to you,
that you may announce the great glad news."
"The Savior of the world is here."

"Go, tell it on the mountain;
over the hills and everywhere."
Tell it in the valleys.
Tell it on the seashore.
Tell it in home and factory,
Tell it in far countries and in near.
Tell it in your own beloved land.
"The Savior of the world is here."

"Listen to him!"
There is no need to remain forever
on the mountain top.
Go down into the valley.
I do not need you to tend the trees and the flowers.
I do not need you to feed the birds,
the squirrel and the deer.

Your calling is to serve people.
People who desperately need to hear the word of life.
I need you
to tend the spiritually sick,
those ignorant of me.
Ignorant of faith, hope, and love.
This is your calling.

I call you out of the world,
not to turn your back on the world,
to withdraw from it,
but to be different from the world
in your commitment

to truth, justice, and peace.
I call you
to give up the ways of the world—
self-centeredness, pride,
greed and lust,
dishonest and unscrupulous ways.

I call you to a new life in Christ.
A clean and pure life,
untrammeled by the wiles and deceit,
the uncleanness of worldly ways.
I call you to holiness,
to a life devoted to my ways—
to honesty and integrity.
I call you to become like my beloved Son,
the One I have placed in your midst.

I call you to emulate him
by your obedience, your commitment,
by your love for people;
my people disenfranchised,
excluded by those ruled by
prejudice and self-righteousness—
the poor,
the lepers of human society.

I call you to bear witness
with heart and hand and voice
to the faith that is in you.
I call you
to testify to the grace and favor of God
shared with you richly in my beloved Son.

Who hears this voice today
out of the heavenly cloud?
Who hears God
above the din, the clatter, the noise
that characterizes our living today?
Are we among the noisemakers,
muffling the voice from the cloud
calling us to our true destiny in life?

Bread? or Crumbs?

Do we still respond to God,
"Here I will remain,
building my booth,
a dwelling for you, for me and no more?
Here I will enshrine you
forever in the place of my choosing."

If this is our response,
we have not heard God.
We have only heard that inner voice
calling us to play at religion,
to seek what is pleasing to our ear.
To continue in a do-it-myself religion
that has no relationship to the voice from the cloud.

I hear a voice,
piercing the armor I have fashioned
to shut out the voice of God.
I hear that voice,
a voice pleading with anxiety and longing
for peace of mind.
A voice crying out for the living God.
I hear the voice of the multitudes
lost in the night,
seeking for truth, hope, and love.

I hear another voice,
the voice from the cloud, pleading,
calling me from my contemplation,
from ease and comfort,
to a life of commitment.

It is the voice of God,
calling like a mighty thunder clap,
commanding,
"Leave your flesh pots,
your couches of ease.
Get on with the work I would have you do."

"Go into the world.
Proclaim the good news,
This is my beloved Son.
Listen to him!
He is the Savior from all grief and pain,
from sin and the powers of death."

"Go!
Be not afraid.
I am with you.
I will be your voice, your strength.
Go where I send you.
Speak what I give you to say.
Go into the valley.
Minister to the hungry,
the homeless,
the lonely,
to all those without the God of Gods.
Go in the name of my Son, my beloved.
Lo, I am with you always."
Amen!

18

The Glory of God

The Tenth Sunday after Pentecost

Psalm 19.1

The heavens are telling the glory
of God;
and the firmament proclaims
his handiwork.

Our Savior's Lutheran Church
Oxnard, California

The Glory of God

In the days of the Psalm writer,
perhaps two and a half thousand years ago,
he gave glory to God
for the wonders of the heavens above
and of the earth beneath.
He had no scientific view
or understanding of these wonders.
Nevertheless he marveled
at the glory of God.

Perhaps we are unjust
to the psalmist.
Perhaps we honor ourselves too much.
We have a scientific understanding and view,
but is there awe and wonder
as we look upon the heavens above
and the earth beneath?

The heavens and the earth
have been reduced to atoms
arranged in mathematical proportions,
in precise equations
through our scientiic view.

Perhaps we know enough
to make us vain and proud
of our knowledge,
but unaware
of the glory and wonder of the universe
in which we live.

Immanuel Kant,
giant philosopher of an earlier generation, said,
"Two things impress me.
Two things attest a creator God:
the starry heavens above
and the moral order within."

The Heavens Above

Look at the heavens on a clear night,
the starry heavens.
How magnificent, how impressive,
their majesty and glory.
Yet we see only a small portion
of the starry heavens as we gaze upwards;
perhaps a few thousand stars at the most.
The stars we see
belong to a galaxy called the Milky Way,
a vast system
composed of more than a hundred billion stars.
Think of the magnitude of the number.

Our galaxy
is like an immense disk.
So vast from end to end that it takes light
one hundred thousand years
to cross from one edge
of our galaxy to another.
Light travels
one hundred eighty-six thousand miles per second.

Our galaxy
at the thickest part of its center
is about ten thousand light years in depth.
This means light travels
from the bottom to the highest point
at the center
for ten thousand years
before reaching the other side
at a speed of
one hundred eighty-six thousand miles per second.

This is but the beginning!
There are hundreds of billions of galaxies in space,
some far larger
than our milky way.
Our nearest galaxy is in the constellation Andromeda,
some two million light years from us.

The Glory of God

Powerful telescopes searching the heavens
have discovered galaxies four billion light years away.
What lies beyond we do not know.
The one who wrote,
"The heavens declare the glory of God,"
knew none of this.
He saw only as far as the human eye could reach.
Nevertheless he was enthralled
by the wonder
and the glory of it.

How can we be smug?
How can we take the heavens so matter-of-factly?
Why do we worship the sun,
the earth, and its creatures,
rather than the creator of it all?

In the beginning
there was only hydrogen,
the simplest of all the elements;
its atom composed of one proton and one electron.
Hydrogen,
so plentiful on our planet earth,
joined to oxygen
to give us water.

Out of the great clouds
of hydrogen in space,
drawn together by the forces of gravity
into denser and denser masses,
came nuclear reactions
as a consequence
of the great heat and pressure
from the close proximity
of trillions of hydrogen atoms.

Nuclear explosions took place.
In fact, scientists believe our universe resulted
from a tremendous explosion

about fifteen billions of years ago.
All the elements of our universe—
oxygen, nitrogen, carbon,
copper, iron, magnesium
calcium, sulfur,
gold, silver, uranium—
were formed
out of these great nuclear explosions.

The mystery is great!
The human mind can penetrate only so far
into the secrets of the past,
into the mystery of the origin of all things.
There is a point
beyond which we cannot pass,
as we seek to unlock the secrets of the universe
that is our home.

Today's Christians,
you and I,
with our vaster knowledge of the universe,
its origins and its magnitude,
have more reason than ever
to give glory to God.

The Earth Beneath

What of the earth beneath?
a unique wonder,
unmatched elsewhere in our vast universe
of which we are a part.
There has been speculation,
and many are convinced,
that other planets in outer space,
planets like our planet earth
likewise have spawned living organisms,
living creatures,
even human life.

The Glory of God

The mathematical possibilities are many
but the probabilities few.
Our planet earth and the life upon it resulted
from unique forces
and unique conditions
that could only rarely be duplicated.
If there are earths like ours
with life upon them,
they would be so far removed from us
that we may never have the means
or the way to communicate
or to travel
from one to the other.

William Pollard,
a modern scientist,
speaking out of experience
and from Christian conviction says,
"The earth
with its breathtaking beauty,
its azure seas, beaches, mighty mountains,
and soft blankets of forest and steppe
is a wonderland in the universe.

It is a gem
of rare and magic beauty
hung in a tractless space
filled with lethal radiations.
Earth is choice,
precious,
and sacred beyond all comparison.
We can only respond with reverence and awe
to such an amazing product
of the creative forces of the universe."

How true this word of the Christian scientist!
This amazing earth
we have from God
as a gift of his benevolence.
How do we use this wondrous gift?

Bread? or Crumbs?

Do we cherish the good earth
out of which we came
and to which at our ending
we return?

Do we cultivate
its beauty and its worth wisely?
We use its resources
wastefully,
selfishly despoiling
and polluting it
out of our greed
and lust for wealth and power.

A trip to the beach,
or a drive on our roadsides,
a nauseous sight
of human garbage and trash
carelessly thrown at will.
A typical example
of our disrespect
for what God has given.
God the giver
deserves better from us!

Now think for a moment
of the thousands, literally millions,
of forms of life
that inhabit this earth.
And in the midst of this plenitude
man and woman!

Fashioned in the image of the Creator,
humans
with marvelous powers
of body, mind, spirit, and will.
What a glory
is each human
who walks in the footsteps
of the Creator!

The Glory of God

How good,
how great we can be when inbreathed
and inspired
by the spirit of our creator God.

Yet how evil, how corrupt,
how wicked,
when inspired by selfishness,
by greed,
and lust for power.
How wickedly we despoil the good earth,
the cradle
in which we are formed.
The cocoon
in which we have our being

Have we doubts
about the existence of God?
Is God remote,
far removed from us?
The universe in which we have our existence
is vast
beyond description.
And God the creator
is above and beyond it all.

Yet he is near!
The great God
who made all and who rules over all
draws near
to lift us out of our morass
of sin and selfishness,
to raise us up
to the glory of his presence.

He is here
in the water in which we were baptized.
He is here
in the bread and in the cup of which we partake.
He is here

Bread? or Crumbs?

to share himself with us,
his good gifts of grace and spirit,
that we may become
the kind of persons in this world
who honor God,
who honor one another,
who honor the good earth,
in our thoughts, our words, and our deeds.

He is here
in these elements from the earth—
the water,
the bread and wine.
He is here
to give himself
that we receive him
to our eternal blessing.

The heavens declare the glory of God
and the earth
is the work of his hands!
This is what I see as I travel the good earth—
the green grass,
the myriad-colored flowers,
the majestic trees,
the towering mountains,
the swift-flowing streams,
the clear lakes,
the waves pounding the shore,

The birds on the wing,
the squirrel darting in the tree,
the chirping of the cricket,
the busy bee and the ant,
the soaring butterfly,
the spirited steed,
the sheep and the goat—
all the animal and mineral kingdom
attest the glory of our creator God.

How can we deny him
who has made us?
How can we live to ourselves alone?
The heavens declare the glory of God.
The earth is the work of his hands.

The Place of God

All of life
interwoven into one web of relationships.
All the vast universe
interdependent,
the one part upon the other.
Each a part of the marvelous web of life
shaped and fashioned
by the creator God.

The poet has said,
"I need not shout my faith!
Thrice eloquent are the green trees
and the quiet listening sod.
Hushed are the stars above
whose powers are never spent,
yet how they speak of God."

We live on an earth of incomparable beauty!
Let us cherish it!
Let us honor, never abuse, it!
Let us hand it down
to our children
and to our children's children
as the great heritage
we have from God.

Let us give glory to him
who has made all this
by living as his stewards
of the good earth.
Let us reflect in all we do
the glory of the Creator,

ever giving honor and praise to him!

> The heavens
> declare the glory of God.
> The earth
> is the work of his hands.
> Let us shout our faith
> by our reverence
> for the starry heavens above
> and for the wondrous earth beneath.
>
> Let us shout our faith
> by our love and concern
> for one another
> and for all who are made
> as we are made
> in the image of our creator God!

19

Not a Sparrow Will Fall

The Fifth Sunday after Pentecost

Matthew 10.26–31

"Have no fear of them; for nothing is covered up that will not be uncovered, and nothing secret that will not become known. What I say to you in the dark, tell in the light; and what you hear whispered, tell from the housetops. Do not fear those who kill the body, but cannot kill the soul; rather fear him who can destroy both soul and body in Gehenna. Are not two sparrows sold for a penny? Yet not one of them will fall to the ground apart from your Father. And even the hairs of our head are all counted. So do not be afraid; you are of more value than many sparrows."

Mountainside Lutheran Church
Robbinsville, North Carolina
July 12, 1981

Not a Sparrow Will Fall

The sparrow!
Not our favorite bird among birds.
Many birds are more attractive
than a sparrow,
beautiful birds
we enjoy and admire.
Who would prefer a sparrow
over a cardinal,
or a bluebird,
or a robin?

Thousands and thousands
of species of birds on planet earth.
Our sparrow
does not make many lists
of favorite birds.

Jesus said,
"Are not two sparrows sold for a penny?"
Evidently sparrows
had little value in Jesus' time.
The most common
of the sparrow family is
the English sparrow,
a nuisance bird
in our book of birds.

The Web of Nature

Nevertheless sparrows
have their place in the web of nature.
They are a part of God's creation.
Jesus said,
"Not a sparrow
will fall to the ground
without your Father's will."
God has a concern for sparrows!
God cares for sparrows too.

Bread? or Crumbs?

It seems to be beneath God
to care for sparrows.
God must have more important things to do.
Would it not be wiser for God
to care for people
than for sparrows?
Jesus is never quoted as saying,
"Not one human
will fall to the ground
without the Father's will."

Are we not more valuable than sparrows?
Many people fall to the ground
every day.
We read or hear about them
in the news or on television.
There were many tragic and unnecessary deaths
yesterday,
and there will be more today.
Little children abused and killed.
Does God love sparrows
more than people?

What a narrow, twisted viewpoint we have.
God is the Creator of all!
God cares for all he has made,
for sparrows and for children.
Our planet earth is teeming with life
of marvelous variety.
Every little spot of ground
alive with life.
Every shovelful of earth
the home of thousands upon thousands
of organisms.

Above the ground and in the air
and in the waters
are creatures of every kind.
Birds
in swift flight through space.

Butterflies
in rich velvet and satin.
Squirrels
leaping from limb to limb in tall trees.
Fish swimming in many waters.

The earth on which we stand
teeming with life—
insects, worms, and microbes
inhabiting the earth, the sky, and the sea.
Each a vital part of the web of life.
Each according to its kind
the object of God's concern and care.

All life on earth interdependent.
The extinction of one species,
even sparrows,
a disaster.
God manifests his loving concern for us
when he cares for sparrows
and for every species of life
on planet earth.

The Lesson

Jesus used the lowly sparrow
as an example
to teach the twelve disciples a lesson
about stewardship
as he sent them forth on their mission
to preach and to heal.
He gave solemn warning
that they would encounter hostility,
contempt, persecution,
even death.

Be certain about your commitment.
No one builds a house
without counting the cost.
Be certain in your hearts and minds

Bread? or Crumbs?

that living and proclaiming
the message of the gospel
is an absolute must.
Count the cost
for there is a price to pay
to be a witness to truth, righteousness,
holiness, and God.

The sparrow is an appropriate example,
for sparrows
are despised, hated,
and efforts have been made
to exterminate them.
So it will be for you when you are faithful
to your calling
to proclaim God's message
of truth and right.

Sparrows continue to thrive and multiply
in spite of every effort
to exterminate them.
So too the message of God
lived and proclaimed by you
will thrive and multiply
in spite of the hatred, the malice,
and the martyrdom of many of you.

God is concerned for the lowly sparrow!
How much greater his concern
for you his faithful witnesses.
"You are of far greater value
than many sparrows."

Fear not!
Let no one deter you from living for God.
Let no one prevent you
from living and speaking the truth
about the immorality and wickedness of people,
even the people of God.
Let justice and truth prevail.

Not a Sparrow Will Fall

Remember the prophets of old
who spoke out fearlessly
about the sins and hypocrisy of God's people.
Martyrdom
is a real prospect for those
who are faithful to the truth of the gospel.
Fear not!
God cares for you.

How often we as disciples of Christ
must make hard and difficult choices.
There was segregation
and integration.
Lynching and murders
from that awful period in our history
are in the news this very day
as a dark and sinful past
continues to haunt us.

There are moral and ethical issues
before us as followers of Jesus daily
about prejudice,
abortion,
sexuality,
same sex marriages,
stem cell research,
war,
treatment of prisoners of war,
treatment of convicts in our prisons,
illegal aliens,
minimum wage,
the unseemly wealth of a few
and the extreme poverty of many,
health care,
pensions,
child abuse,
sexual harassment,
ownership of assault weapons
and the proliferation of the gun mentality,
pornography,

Bread? or Crumbs?

gambling as a source of revenue
for church and state,
status of women in the work place,
HIV and aids,
the rape of our environment.
The list goes on and on.

As followers of Jesus,
we must make difficult choices daily.
How much easier to be silent,
to avoid controversy,
to place our light under a bushel.
How difficult to speak out as Amos the prophet,
"Let justice roll down like waters,
and righteousness like an ever-flowing stream."

How timid we are about genuine stewardship,
of responsibility to God
for sharing the abundance we have
with those who have so little.
I do not know what tomorrow will bring.
They got themselves into their predicament.
My little gift will not go far.
God's requirement
is always that we sin on the side of love,
to go out on a limb,
to do the right thing,
to empathize with those who suffer wrong,
injustice, poverty.

There is always a frontier
before us
beyond the protective walls we have built
to shield ourselves
from the real world of poverty,
of prejudice,
of injustice,
of the suffering and tragedy of many,
to hide the hurts and wounds
of others from our eyes.

The frontier
is enemy territory.
For God has many enemies out there
who hate his word of truth,
love and justice.
Love interferes with our selfish goals,
the pursuit of our own enrichment
at the expense of others.

Love
places its compulsion upon us
to stand up and be counted
when hate,
falsehood,
injustice,
and prejudice
squeeze life out of another human.

There are risks
to be a Christian in the world.
Jesus never said
sparrows will not fall to the ground.
He said,
"Your heavenly Father knows;
He cares."

There is an alternative far worse
than mere survival in the world.
What kind of person am I
in my own eye
when I compromise the truth,
or deny the faith,
or live a lie?
I am aware of the kind of person I am
in the eye of God.
But who am I
in my innermost self?

Bread? or Crumbs?

Is there self-respect
issuing from the knowledge
that God has created me in his own image
to be like him
in my respect and love
for even the least
and even the worst member of the human family?

God is always at work
through our Lord Jesus
and through his Word and Spirit
to redeem and renew
all creation
and every member of the human family.
He works through you and me.
We are the disciples
sent forth to proclaim good news,
to heal the sick,
to give sight to the blind,
to restore a lost and fallen humanity
to love and peace and holiness.

We do so at great risk.
We may fall to the ground
because of the hatred and enmity
of those who wallow in their wickedness.
Those who are blinded
by the gods of this world.
We may even become victims of good people
who are affronted
by our commitment
to truth and justice and equality.
Good people who believe
they have a corner on the knowledge
of God's will and purpose.

Was it not good people,
religious people,
who were most critical of Jesus' deeds and words,
who brought about his death?

Doing God's will,
sharing God's word with others,
living a life of love and faithfulness to God
does not spare us
from the risk of falling to the ground.

God has abundantly blessed us
with far more of this world's goods
than are needed for our livelihood.
He gives generously
and he invites us to give and share that
the hungry be fed,
the naked clothed,
the homeless sheltered
the enslaved set free.

The Witness

Why has God created you and me?
Is it not to be his people in the world?
to live for him,
to speak for him,
to tend and care for the good earth,
to love and share
our many blessings with the have nots?
to declare his wonderful deeds
to people everywhere?

To be, as the Apostle Paul wrote
to the Corinthians,
the aroma of Christ,
a fragrance of a sweet smell
to those who are being saved
and also to those who are perishing?

There is risk and danger
when we speak boldly in behalf of
truth and righteousness,
justice and love.
But there is a far greater danger:

Bread? or Crumbs?

to be silent
when we should have championed the cause
of right and justice and truth.
To deny the God who has made us.
To exploit and use people
to our advantage.
To be dishonest and selfish.
To worship God with our lips,
but with hearts
in love with pleasure, wealth, and power.

We are always in peril
because of the dominating force of our ego,
our inner selfishness,
which places our will and desire
above the call of God.
This disease
is common to every human,
to every one of us,
and is always fatal in the end
when ego rules us and not Christ.

To be self-centered is
to fall to the ground
like a sparrow,
unmourned and soon forgotten.
Jesus said,
"Do not fear those who kill the body,
but have no power
to destroy your spiritual life,
your relationship to God.

Rather be afraid of the one
who can destroy both soul and body in Gehenna."
Gehenna!
the dump outside Jerusalem
where trash was always burning.
Be afraid, said Jesus,
lest you end up in the trash
rather than in the holy city of God.

Life without God at the center
is Gehenna,
a dead end without the loving God
who saves
from the treachery of a selfish heart.

Discipleship
is challenging and dangerous.
There are enemies
who can do great bodily harm
to the people of God.
Jesus challenged his disciples not to fear.
Behold, the sparrow.
God cares for them.
How much more he cares for you.

There will never be an end to sparrows
for God cares for them.
How much more God cares for you.
Our life in Christ
is secure,
for God is the faithful God,
true to his promise,
"Lo, I am with you always."

Baptized into Christ!
Born to be Christian!
Created to be a witness for the Gospel of God.
Shaped and molded
by word and sacrament
to be living, walking signs
of the grace and mercy of God in the world.
Sent forth
to proclaim everywhere
and especially in the community
where we have our home,
God's message of truth, justice, and love.

Let us go forth
in the name of Christ

to share the good news
with people everywhere.

Let us go forth
with courage and enthusiasm.
Let us go in love,
loving the loveless,
ministering to those wounded
by hatred,
prejudice and exploitation.

Let us go to those enslaved
to lust and greed,
to substance abuse,
to love of money,
and to bondage to this world's goods.

We have good news!
The good news Jesus proclaimed.
The message for which he lived and died.
God loves you.
God cares for you.
No evil can befall you
that can separate you from the love of God.

Sparrows
have little or no value
to people.
Yet God cares for them.
Does he not care
much more for you?
Why be anxious?
Why be fearful and timid?
Let us go forth with courage and daring.
Let us go forth with a song on our lips
and love in our hearts,
a song of thanksgiving and praise
that God has called us to discipleship.
To be a part of his great mission—
the redemption of the world
and of all mankind.

20

Peace or a Sword?

The Sixth Sunday after Pentecost

Matthew 10.34–39

"Do not think that I have come to bring peace to the earth; I have not come to bring peace, but a sword. For I have come to set a man against his father, and a daughter against her mother, and a daughter-in-law against her mother-in-law; and one's foes will be members of one's own household.
Whoever loves father or mother more than me is not worthy of me; and whoever loves son or daughter more then me is not worthy of me; and whoever does not take up the cross and follow me is not worthy of me. Those who find their life will lose it, and those who lose their life for my sake will find it."

St. Andrew Lutheran Church
Andrews, North Carolina
June 25, 1978

Peace or a Sword?

Peace on earth
has been the fervent prayer of many
since the beginning
of the history of humankind.
Yet history is the story of war,
bloodshed, and destruction.
Not peace!

Wars and bloody conflicts
rage in Iraq
and Afghanistan.
We all feel the pain,
especially those who have lost loved ones.
Israel and the Palestinians.
Russia and Chechyna.
The Sudan.
India and Pakistan.
Drug wars in Mexico,
and South American countries.
Gang wars
in many of our major cities.

The emphasis upon
military budgets
in our United States and many countries
has placed a fearful burden
of debt upon us
and is even a threat to planet earth.
Huge amounts of money
for war,
but not one penny to promote peace.
We do not know
how to resolve our differences
through negotiation.
When conflicts arise,
we take up the sword;
not the olive branch of peace.
Peacemaking

is a sign of weakness,
not of strength—
nationally, internationally,
and even domestically.

Peace on Earth

How do we as Christians
settle our differences with other Christians?
Is it peace or the sword?
Christians
are embroiled in conflict and strife
with one another.

The great, devastating wars
of the past century
were waged by nations we call Christian.
We have a sorry record
of crusades and religious wars.

We celebrate the birthday of Jesus annually,
the one we call the Prince of Peace.
We glorify in music
the immortal words of the heavenly host,
"Peace on earth
to people of good will."
We are deeply moved emotionally
by these words.
But as we return to daily life in the world,
we leave peace at the church door
and return to the strife and conflict
that mar our daily life.

We pray for peace,
but we promote war and conflict.
We insist on our way.
We antagonize one another
by our words and actions.
We look down on those we consider
inferior.

We take advantage and exploit and use
people for our own ends.

Is peace on earth
only a dream, or a shibboleth
we speak glibly?
Or is peace a genuine possibility
in our lives and in our time?

The Sword

Jesus said,
"Do not think that I have come
to bring peace on earth.
I have not come to bring peace,
but a sword.

What strange words
from the mouth of the Prince of Peace.
Words that contradict
the image we have of our Lord Jesus.
We believe he came
to bring peace.
How then could he say,
"I have not come to bring peace,
but a sword?"

Are we wrong about the one we call
the Prince of Peace?
Search the Scriptures,
both the ancient writings of the prophets
and our New Testament.
The message is of reconciliation.
The resurrected Lord said to his disciples,
"Peace I leave with you.
My peace I give to you.
Not as the world gives do I give to you."

Then this incomprehensible word,
"I came not to bring peace,

but a sword."
When we read the gospels carefully,
we discover
Jesus was not always a peaceful man.
Righteous indignation
led him to drive the moneychangers
out of the temple.

He spoke strong words
of condemnation
against the religious leaders.
"You offspring of vipers!
You hypocrites!
Woe to you!
Full of extortion and rapacity.
You blind Pharisees!
You are like whitewashed tombs.
Beautiful on the outside,
but full of hypocrisy and iniquity.
Woe to you!
who persecute and kill and crucify
prophets, wise men,
and scribes sent from God."

Do these sayings sound like the words
of a peaceful man?
He also warned those
who caused little children to sin,
"It is better
that a great millstone
be hanged about your neck
and you be drowned
in the depth of the sea."

What did Jesus mean
when he said,
"I came not to bring peace,
but a sword?"
Jesus was not a military man.
He never carried a sword.
He did not defend himself against his accusers.

His followers said of him
when he was reviled,
He did not revile in return.
When he suffered,
he did not threaten.
But he also said,
"I came not to bring peace,
but a sword."

The Nature of the Gospel

The gospel is good news!
It is the message
of God's love and compassion
for us,
for sinners.
For those described in the pages of scripture
as lost and condemned persons.

We are enemies of God!
We are by nature alienated from him,
so that we seek our own
in everything we do.
We are lost
and under condemnation.
We are enslaved to sin and selfishness.
Sin and selfishness
that lead to death.

Our gracious God
comes in love and pity
to deliver us from sin and selfishness,
from the powers of evil,
from death.
How joyful we should be.
How we should lift our voices
in praise and thanksgiving.

BREAD? OR CRUMBS?

But we resist God.
We respond in a half-hearted,
lukewarm way.
In my youth
a new pastor came
to one of the Lutheran churches
in our community.
He was a warm loving man,
dedicated to God
and to people.
He began some innovations,
programs that had not been done
in our community.

Bible study groups for young people,
for women,
and a group for men.
He went after people
with the gospel
in a very direct way.

There was the town barber,
supposedly a church member
who rarely attended,
and whose reputation was a bit unsavory—
gambling, bootlegging
were his tricks in trade.
He resisted.
He tried to avoid the pastor.

There was war and no peace.
He fought with all his strength
against the gospel of God.
I heard him tell his story.
How the battle raged within him.
How the gospel overcame his resistance.
How he became
a dedicated child of God.

Peace or a Sword?

There was a farmer
equally determined to hold the Lord Jesus
at arm's length.
Satisfied with church membership
and a work righteousness
who believed he had done enough.
for his own salvation.
He avoided meeting the pastor personally.
But the pastor
cornered him in the field
as he cultivated corn.
He resisted.
He fought with all his strength.

The gospel
of the Prince of Peace
overcame his hostility towards God.
This was where and when
he yielded his sword
and bent his knee
to the Prince of Peace.
This is what Jesus meant
when he said,
"Do not think that I have come
to bring peace on earth.
I have come not to bring peace
but a sword."

The gospel attacks us
laying bare our hostility to God.
Breaking down the barriers
we have erected
against a closer walk with him.
The barriers!
The excuses we make.
I'm good enough the way I am.
I do not do anything really bad.
I do the best I can.

Bread? or Crumbs?

But deep inside
we hear the still small voice
of the accuser.
God wants you.
The total you.
Not just the outer shell.
But your heart and mind and life
in total commitment
to his will for your life.

God calls us to total commitment.
God would set us free
from divided loyalties.
From an appearance of righteousness
and Christian commitment.
From a life
that has an appearance of godliness,
but is really anchored
in the pleasures
and treasures of this world.

How we resist!
How many the excuses we offer.
We even bargain with God.
God,
if you will do this for me,
I will do that for you.

Jesus did not come to bring
a false peace,
a cheap grace
that says we are good enough
just as we are.
He came with a sword
To slash away our excuses
and the security blankets
we have carefully built
to protect ourselves
from the challenge of the gospel.
The challenge

that says we must die daily to self and sin
and rise daily to the new life
of faith and devotion to God's will.

The gospel
is sharper than any two-edged sword,
says the word of God.
The word of the cross
pierces to the deepest level
of our self,
laying bare the true picture
of what we are in our hearts and minds.

The Divider

The gospel
is like a sword in another way too.
The gospel divides us
one from another.
When the gospel throws
its powerful net over us
and captures us for God,
someone we love will be threatened.

Resistance to God
is in the heart and mind
of each one of us.
How wonderful, how blessed
when the gospel brings us
and our dear ones together in Christ.

But it is not always so.
Sometimes allegiance to Christ
causes a division in the family.
A wife and a husband.
A father and son,
A mother and daughter.
A sister and brother.
One has found peace in Christ.
The other has not.

Bread? or Crumbs?

Sometimes the divisions run deep.
So it was between
my father and my mother
when I was a youngster.
There was conflict
over church attendance and commitment.

But mother was strong.
Her commitment was total.
She persisted in her loyalty to Christ
and to her church
in spite of the negativism of my father.
She gathered us about her
at the close of each day
for the reading of God's word
and for prayer.

Then one evening Dad came,
took the Bible from her,
and led us in reading and prayer.
No longer was there war.
There was peace.
The sword was no more,
for Christ had gained Dad's heart.
Mother's steadfastness
and patience
had won the match
and we were united as a family in Christ.

The gospel
is the message of peace.
But the gospel is also a sword
severing us
from all the supports and security blankets
we have used
to put God in a little cubbyhole in our life.

The gospel
is the message of peace.

Peace or a Sword?

But the gospel is also a sword
dividing us from dear ones,
from one another.
What shall we do in such a time?
How we respond
is critical for our faith and life.

If we hide our light
under a basket.
If we knuckle under to our dear one,
there can be no peace
with God.
God has called us to let our light shine,
to bear witness to the faith
that is in us.

Faith
is to place God first
above every loyalty and commitment.
Faith is to live
as though there were no tomorrows.
Today is God's day for us to live
in God's peace and love.
We are called by our Lord
to be witnesses
to his grace and favor
in every moment
by our deeds, our words,
and our attitude towards life.

God's radical makeover of us
from self-centered,
worldly-minded people
to God-centered,
Spirit-filled people
comes only with a total commitment.

When this happens to us,
then change
will come to our dear ones,

not through the power of the sword,
through threat and intimidation,
but through God's gift of peace,
through patient steadfastness in Christ.

We are at peace,
even when a sword hangs over our heads,
for our lives
are anchored in Christ.
No threat, no trouble,
no fear
can destroy the peace and joy
we know in our hearts
when our life is hid with Christ in God.

"Blessed are you,"
said our Lord,
"for whoever loses his or her life
for my sake has found it."

21

Where to Find Bread?

The Tenth Sunday after Pentecost

John 6.1–15

After this Jesus went to the other side of the Sea of Galilee, also called the Sea of Tiberias. A large crowd kept following him because they saw the signs that he was doing for the sick. Jesus went up the mountain and sat down there with his disciples. Now the Passover, the festival of the Jews was near. When he looked up and saw a large crowd coming toward him, Jesus said to Philip, "Where are we to buy bread for these people to eat?" He said this to test him, for he himself knew what he was going to do. Philip said to him, "Six months wages would not buy enough bread for each of them to get a little. One of his disciples, Andrew, Simon Peter's brother said to him, "There is a boy here who has five barley loaves and two fish. But what are they among so many people?" Jesus said, "Make the people sit down." Now there was a great deal of grass in the place; so they sat down, about five thousand in all. Then Jesus took the loaves, and when he had given thanks, he distributed them to those who were seated; so also the fish, as much as they wanted. When they were satisfied, he told his disciples, "Gather up the fragments left over, so that nothing may be lost." So they gathered them up, and from the fragments of the five barley loaves left by those who had eaten, they filled twelve baskets. When the people saw the sign that he had done. they began to say, "This is indeed the prophet who is to come into the world."

St. Andrew Lutheran Church
Andrews, North Carolina
August 12, 1979

Where to Find Bread?

Bread lines
in the thirties.
How many of us remember those days?
We were on a farm in Minnesota.
There was plenty of bread.
Thousands, even millions
suffered hunger in those days.
Unemployment,
Drought,
The dust bowl,
Failed banks.
Many suffered a lack of bread.

The war years of the Forties.
Many scavenged garbage cans
for a piece of bread.
They searched for even a crust
to assuage hunger.
Bread has been a basic food
in all times and in all places.

The year 2003.
Food pantries. Soup kitchens.
The homeless
living under bridges,
sleeping on the streets
in our rich land.
In many a poor nation millions
malnourished,
starving, dying
for lack of bread
and for the essentials for life.

We see and hear of their sad plight
on the media.
Members of our human family
in Africa,
Sudan, Ethiopia.

Bread? or Crumbs?

And in Asia—
China, Afghanistan, North Korea.
To mention only a few.

The French novelist,
Victor Hugo,
authored a book, *Les Miserables*.
A story of a poor man,
Jean Valjean.
Orphaned in childhood.
Living with a widowed sister,
the mother of seven children.
Jean became the support
of the family.
Times were hard.
The winter severe.
Jean unemployed.
There was no bread for seven hungry children.
On a Sunday eve
the baker heard glass shatter
in his shop window.
A man had shattered the glass
with his fist
Jean had stolen a loaf of bread
to feed seven hungry children.

The punishment:
five years in the galleys at hard labor.
All for a loaf of bread.
The galleys:
A hell hole for humans.
His sentence
increased to nineteen years
for attempts to escape.
All for a loaf of bread
stolen to feed seven hungry children.

Where to Find Bread?

A Multitude without Bread

In the time of Jesus
many lacked bread.
One day Jesus went to the far side
of the Sea of Galilee.
To an isolated place.
He went up on a mountain
With his disciples
A large crowd followed him.
It was Passover time.
Jesus knew
the people had no bread.

He said to Philip,
"Where are we to find bread
for these people to eat?'
Philip said,
"Two hundred denarii,
Six months wages would not buy enough bread
for each of them to have a little piece."
One denarius—a day's wage
for a laborer.

Where to find bread?
They were far from the marketplace.
But even a market
could not supply enough bread
for this multitude of people.

Where to find bread?
Andrew said,
"There is a boy here with
five barley loaves
and two fish.
But what is this for so many people?"
Five loaves
Hardly a crumb for each person.

Jesus took the loaves,
Gave thanks,
Broke them,

Bread? or Crumbs?

and gave to the people.
They all ate and were satisfied.
Marvel of marvels!
Twelve baskets remained over
when everyone had eaten.

Compare this
to the hungry multitudes today.
Dreadful stories of hunger,
starvation,
in many lands on planet Earth.
Even in our own rich land.
Dreadful stories of hunger,
starvation,
disease, and death
because of the lack of bread.

There is no bread!
There is no Jesus
to multiply a few loaves into plenty
to feed hungry multitudes.
This is the sad story of our times.
Modern communications
bring us in touch
with every part of our globe daily.
We know the sad story
of hungry, starving, dying people
because there is no bread.

What to do?
Can we speak a word over our bread
and multiply a few loaves
into plenty for the hungry multitudes?
Did not Jesus say,
"Greater works shall you do
because I go to the Father?"

Why do we lack power
to give bread to the hungry multitudes?
Should not we who bear the name of Christ

Where to Find Bread?

in his name
supply bread
for the hungry people of the world?

The Heart of the Story

What happened that day
on a mountain in an uninhabited region
that five loaves of bread became a meal
for five thousand?

The easy answer given by many today,
Jesus was God.
Jesus had the power of God.
God can do whatever he pleases.
Since Jesus was God even one loaf
would have been enough to feed
five thousand.

If this is so,
Why does not God feed the hungry multitudes today?
Why do men, women, children,
especially little children,
starve for lack of bread?

Are they not precious to God?
If God has the power
Why does he not relieve us of the curse of
hunger, starvation,
sickness and death?

If God did this
once upon a time,
Why not today and every day?
Why does not God rid our world of
hunger, drought,
starvation, and death?

This is not what this story of
the five thousand is all about.

Bread? or Crumbs?

This story is a mirror of the human situation
of our human condition.
This is the story of the entire human family.
Empty inside,
hungry, starving, dying
Because there is no God in our life
greater than
the god of self,
The god we have created out of bread
to be our God.

We are hungry
with an insatiable hunger
that no earthly bread can satisfy.
A hunger
common to every member
of the human family.
A hunger for the living God.
For the God
who has created us,
Who has fashioned out of rude clay
a person of mind,
spirit, and will.
A person of unlimited capacity for
love, goodness,
and growth
in all that is good, noble, and true.

We have sold our birthright
for a mess of pottage.
We seek the answer for our deep hunger in
wealth,
power,
pleasure,
luxury, and ease.

But this bread can never satisfy.
This bread is not the answer
to the human problem of
greed, envy,

Where to Find Bread?

hatred, lust,
selfishness, and death.

This bread upon which we feed
is the kiss of death for the people
who know not God.
Our sickness is unto death.
We strive for bread that cannot satisfy.
For bread that blinds our eye
and deafens our ear
to truth,
and to the voice of God

We are empty inside.
The bread upon which we feed
can never satisfy that deep hunger
within our being.
We are from God, his handiwork.
Fashioned, molded
out of the dust of the ground
into living beings.
Living beings
fashioned and molded in the image of God.

We toil and strive,
We scheme and plan,
We save and lay up security for our future.
A future
that never comes to pass because we are mortal.
Subject to disease,
death, and decay.

Was it for this
God raised us out of the dust of the ground?
Are we only grass alive today
and gone tomorrow?
No! There is an eternity to this dust
Shaped and molded by God
into form and substance
into which he breathed the breath of life.

Eternity, however,
is not inherent to clay.
Eternity does not belong to the nature of dust.
Only to the dust
inbreathed, inspirited
by the breath of the living God.

That hunger
deep within us is not for things.
That hunger is for God, for the living God.
We hunger for bread,
for the living bread that comes down from heaven.
We hunger
for God's gift of the Savior,
for Jesus who fed the hungry multitude
on a mountainside with living bread,
the bread of life.

The Bread of Life

There is one who comes.
He is here.
He comes from God to us.
To answer our need.
To satisfy our hunger.
There is nothing in his hand.
Yet from his hand we are marvelously fed.
For that man Jesus
Took the loaves,
Gave thanks,
Broke them
and gave to the people.
They ate and were satisfied.
For whoever partakes of the living God
finds the answer for that deep longing,
that yearning within
to be whole.

The gospel
of the feeding of the five thousand is

Where to Find Bread?

God's good news to us
in the language of symbol and figure.
There is no need
to claim divine powers for Jesus
over nature's ways.
Power to multiply five loaves into enough bread
to satisfy the physical hunger of
five thousand people.
That was not their salvation.

The gospel
is always the message of salvation
from sin, death,
and the powers of evil.
The gospel is not a word about the satisfaction
of our physical desires,
of our yearnings
for more of the crumbs of this life,
so that we find security from poverty, want,
and pleasure
in the abundance of things.

If Jesus fed five thousand
only with bread baked in our ovens
made of wheat flour or rye
then the gospel
has no meaning and purpose for us.
For in a few hours
the five thousand
were hungry for more of the same.

Five loaves do not the gospel make.
The Gospel is good news.
the good news that God comes in Jesus
to deliver us
from that inner hunger that binds us
to this world,
to the world of things
and causes us to lose out on the life of the Spirit.
the eternal life
for which we have been created by God.

Bread? or Crumbs?

Jesus came from God
with good news
of our origins and of our destiny.
With the good news
God has come to deliver us
from that hunger that is always fatal in the end.

The gospel is good news
that frees us from our dependence
upon this world's bread.
In this word
the truth of God is imaged.
We see ourselves
Our sad plight,
our deep need.
Our helplessness and hopelessness without God.

In this Gospel we see God
The living God, the loving God,
who comes in Jesus
to save us
from every threat to our eternity.

God comes to give life:
Life filled with blessing, life abundant,
Life overflowing with the gifts of the Spirit—
Love, Joy, Peace,
Goodness, Contentment;
Humility, Patience, Kindness,
Generosity, Faithfulness,
Gentleness,
Self-control.
These are never the fruits of the bread
we eat at our tables
but only at the table of our Lord.

This is the bread Jesus gave
that day to hungry people on a mountainside.
This is the bread Jesus gives

to his people today as we gather
to partake and to celebrate
at the table of our Lord.

The Purpose of This Gift of Bread

Why do we eat?
Is it for ourselves alone?
Do we not eat that we,
the people of God,
may find purpose and "meaning for life."
That we like Jesus on the mountainside
will share the bread of life
with those who "have no bread."

What is our mission?
What is our purpose here?
To eat and to be satisfied that we have been fed?
There is a much greater reason.
We come to the table of our Lord
to be empowered
to share the bread of life
with those who have not.

There are many on our doorstep
and in the many corners of this land
who are starving, dying because they feed only
upon the crumbs
of wealth, power, pleasure
who have never tasted and eaten the bread of life.

Where to find bread for the hungry multitudes today?
Where else but here?
Here God shares the good news of the gospel with us.
Here we share in the bread that Jesus takes
blesses, breaks,
and gives to us
to eat that we may live forever.

Bread? or Crumbs?

But above all
Given and shed
that we, inbreathed and inspirited by the living God,
may go forth
from his table today
to share the bread of life so freely given
and so freely received
with the hungry multitudes who know not God.

For this purpose
and for this reason only
God calls us the body of Christ on earth to give
our body and our blood
for the salvation of our brothers and sisters
around the world
who know not God.

22

A Journey into Faith

The Fifteenth Sunday after Pentecost

Matthew 19.10–12

His disciples said to him, "If such is the case of a man with his wife, it is better not to marry." But he said to them, "Not everyone can accept this teaching, but only those to whom it is given. For there are eunuchs who have been so from birth, and there are eunuchs who have been made eunuchs by others, and there are eunuchs who have made themselves eunuchs for the sake of the kingdom of heaven. Let anyone accept this who can."

Holy Cross Lutheran Church
Fairfield, Ohio
September 17, 2006

A Journey into Faith

I had a dream.
A powerful dream.
A dream so powerful that I awakened
to relate my dream
with great detail and order
to my dear wife Viola.

There was a gathering of the saints
to consider enrollment
for young people in one of our Bible camps.
The leader was persuasive,
but one young lady
was negative.
There would be gays and lesbians
at the camp.
She wanted no part of such a fellowship.

A young man arose to defend her.
Quoting Scripture is a favorite pastime
for those who read our Bible
selectively.
We can always find passages
in Scripture
that support our favorite viewpoint
whatever it might be.

I was startled and amazed
at the ferociousness of the response
to the leader of the discussion.
I said,
"I did not intend to become involved
in this discussion,
but I cannot be silent."
And here is what I said.

I was once like you
in my thoughts and attitudes
towards people who are different.

I was either indifferent to them
or deeply prejudiced.
This is our natural inclination—
to be self-righteous and proud.
To be superior.
To look down upon those
who are not created in our image.

Reason Number One

There are three reasons why
I cannot be silent.
First, I believe with all my heart
what our patron saint, Martin Luther,
wrote in the Small Catechism
in his explanation
of the First Article of the Apostles' Creed:
"I believe
that God has created me
and all that exists."

I am not what I am
because I have done a great work
of creating myself.
I am what I am
because God has given me
a multitude of gifts and talents
that are beyond
any human effort to create or compose.

Then by his grace
he has placed me in an environment
where I have had the privilege
of developing and using
these gifts and talents
in positive and constructive ways.

We are not equal at birth.
Some have great potential.
Others have far less.

A Journey into Faith

Some are born into a good home
with all the resources
to develop a full and productive life.
Many, many others are born
into the worst kind of an environment
where they are conditioned
from birth
to all that is self-destructive.

Did God create gays and lesbians
to be what they are?
Or are they self-created?
Did God create a child with spina bifida?
Or are they created by human parents?
Who has willed to bring children
into the world
without fingers or limbs?
with a lack of mental capacities?
with physical deficiencies
of a rare and stultifying kind?

Is it true that God has created me
and all that exists?
or is it not true?
Does God make mistakes?
Or is creation still evolving
as the handiwork of God?

The mystery is great.
Beyond the powers of human minds to fathom.
But if God is the creator
of all that exists,
then there is purpose and meaning.
We have been given the solemn calling
to find purpose and meaning
in the lives of those
who are not created in our image:
strong, healthy,
endowed with great gifts of mind and spirit.

It is our calling to receive with compassion
and love
those who are different:
the weak, the deficient,
those who are oriented differently sexually.
We are not,
as the Apostle says,
to look differently upon
"the Greek and the Jew,
the slave and the free,
the male and the female."
Yet this is what we do consciously
and subconsciously.

Jesus, our Lord,
made no distinction between
rich and poor,
the righteous and sinners,
good and bad people.
He made no comment upon
heterosexuality or homosexuality
except in one passage
according to Matthew,
"There are those who are eunuchs from birth,
There are those who have been made eunuchs by others,
and there are those who have made themselves eunuchs
for the sake of the kingdom of God."

He said,
"I came to save those who are lost."
This was his great mission in life.
He was faithful and true
to his calling from God.
He has charged us with that mission
to go forward
with the great task
of reconciling every human on earth to God.

A Journey into Faith

Reason Number Two

Luther continues in Article Number Two,
"I believe that Jesus Christ
has redeemed me,
a lost and condemned creature."
By grace alone and by faith alone,
which are God's creation in my heart,
have I been changed
from self-righteousness and pride
into a genuine human being
created in the image of God;
a human who can receive and welcome
into full communion
another human who is not created in my image.

What would I be
apart from this grace from God
that has been shared so generously with *me*
through the suffering and death
of my Lord Jesus?
I would be ruled by all the passions
of the human spirit:
pride, self-righteousness,
envy, greed, lust, anger, malice,
selfishness, love of money,
dishonesty, unfaithfulness.
Name it!
I would be guilty.

But thanks be to God.
I have been set free from this bondage.
Not that I am perfect,
for the potential is always there
for each and every one of these anti-human attitudes
to come to expression in my life.
And they do!
But God has not left me helpless
in a hopeless situation.

Reason Number Three

Luther continues in the Third Article,
"The Holy Spirit has called *me*
through the Gospel,
enlightened *me* with his gifts,
and sanctified and preserved *me*
in the true faith."

I would be Failure Number One
without the presence of God in my life.
There is the calling,
the enlightenment,
the sanctification,
and the preservation in faith
that is entirely the gift of God's grace to *me*.

This was the gift of God to *me*
in my baptism.
Given once and for all time to me,
but never an isolated incident in my life
once upon a time.

For the devil is always present
to tempt me and to lead me
back into that condition of life
where I have no god but the god of self.
A self that gives expression
to all the human expressions
of wickedness and evil
that is in all of us.

Who is this devil?
Not some evil spiritual personality out there.
That devil is right here
in my self, my ego.
I am my own devil.
I am the one who seeks to go my own way,
to let pride and self-righteousness
rule my heart

rather than the God who created me,
redeemed me,
and sanctified me in faith.

How can I hate another human being
created in the image of God
as I am created?
How can I despise another human being
created in the image of God
as I am created?
This is what I do apart from the grace of God.

This is why Luther also wrote
about our baptism,
"The old Adam in us (the devil)
must be drowned and destroyed
by daily sorrow and repentance
and be put to death,
that the new man in Christ may come forth
and live daily to the glory of God."

God is love!
God is not hate!
This is the resounding theme
throughout our New Testament.
God hates no one,
however misguided, evil, or self-righteous
we may be.
He loves us,
for he has created *you* and *me*.
He has redeemed *us*,
and he has given *us* his loving
and powerful Spirit
to change us into his image of love.

We are not love
until the Spirit of God abides in us
motivating and energizing us
to receive every human being
as our equal,

and more than our equal.
For there are we but for the grace of God.

Whenever there is hate in our hearts,
or a despising of another
because they do not measure up to our standards
of what a human should be,
it is an expression of the devil within us.
God save us from ourselves!

My faith journey
has taken me from a narrow-minded bigot
to an open-mindedness
to all that God has created.
I am not free, however,
from my past,
from my self.
There is this daily struggle
to live up to the ideal that God desires
every one of us to become
by his grace and favor.

Our prayer must always be,
"God help *me*
to be this day what you will for me to be.
Save me from myself
that I may this day share in the gifts
of your grace and glory
and that I may share these gifts
of grace and glory
with every one I meet today."

23

Treasure and the Heart

Matthew 6.19–21

"Do not store up for yourselves treasures on earth, where moth and rust consume, and where thieves break in and steal; but store up for yourselves treasures in heaven, where neither moths and rust consumes and where thieves do not break in and steal. For where your treasure is, there your heart will be also."

Treasure and the Heart

Treasure!
Gold has been precious since ancient times.
Humans have striven,
have lived and died
for the love of gold.
Gold is precious today;
more than four hundred dollars a troy ounce.
Investors have made fortunes.
Some have lost everything,
even life,
in the quest for gold.

In our lesson Jesus links treasure and the heart.
The heart!
A mighty muscle
weighing little more than half a pound.
Beating!
Constantly beating!
Seventy times a minute.
Four thousand two hundred times an hour.
One hundred thousand,
eight hundred times a day.
Thirty six million,
seven hundred ninety two thousand times a year.
How many beats in a heart
through a lifetime!

What a mighty organ
the heart!
Pumping blood through one hundred thousand miles
of blood vessels.
Every twelve hours the heart
expends enough energy
to lift sixty-five tons,
that is, one hundred thirty thousand pounds
one foot off the ground.
What astounding figures!

The heart!
The workhorse of all our organs.
The heart!
The center of our affections and our emotions.
We love with the heart.
The sensations of fear, hate, elation, joy
surge through our hearts.

Our heart!
Always on duty as long as we live.
Constantly,
continually beating
to keep us in life.
Our heart
always playing a dual role—
ever working for our survival
and always interested in treasure.

The Yearning for Treasure

Jesus said,
"Where your treasure is,
there your heart will be also."
What a true observation,
for our attention, our affection, and our love
can be fixed
only and always upon treasure.

There is a treasure
which is to take precedence over every other
in our heart's affections.
Jesus calls this
"the treasure in heaven."
A treasure that never fails;
where no thief can rob
or no moth destroy.

What a strange saying
in the mouth of our Lord!

Treasure and the Heart

"Sell your possessions and give to charity!"
Sell all the treasure
we hold dear and give to the poor.
Do not lay up treasure on earth.

What would we do without our treasure?
Treasure
provides security, comfort, strength, well-being.
Who can take Jesus seriously
when he says,
"Sell your possessions and give to the poor?"

We must have treasure;
otherwise we could not survive.
How foolish of Jesus
to make this a condition of Christian life!
Our immediate reaction?
I will follow you, Lord,
but not this proviso.
There are many readers of scripture
who claim
that Jesus' teachings are to be taken literally.

Yet everyone of us has flunked this command.
There was a rich man
who came to Jesus seeking
the security of eternal life.
Jesus said,
"Go, sell all that you have
and give to the poor."

The man went away sorrowful.
His treasure was dear to him;
too dear to sell and give away.
We would have reacted in the same way.
In fact,
we have all reacted in the same way.
For PBP
(pocket book protection),
the natural instinct governing every one of us

has always won the day
in the contest between treasure and charity.

Is it possible,
is it realistic to take Jesus' saying literally?
What would be the result?
We have helped the poor,
but we have become poor in so doing.
His command is impractical.
How could he have said such a thing?

The saying, however, is a mirror,
a reflection of his own life.
Day by day
he traveled the land.
He taught.
He ministered to the spiritual needs of people.
He was fed and nourished
through the goodness and kindness
of those who believed in him.

What would be the situation
if everyone of us became his kind of follower?
If everyone of us
sold our possessions and gave to the poor?
We will never know,
for we are not about to practice what he preached.

The Meaning of Treasure

Jesus was a radical.
He often spoke radically
to capture the attention of his audience.
He said,
"Love your enemy.
If anyone takes your coat, give him your shirt also.
Pray for those who abuse you.
Forgive those who sin against you."

Treasure and the Heart

"Sell your possessions and give to the poor"
is one of his radical pronouncements.
Should we take it literally?
Perhaps not!
Should we take it seriously?
Emphatically, "Yes!"

Jesus' principal concern
in all his teaching
is the inner condition of our heart and spirit.
We are each of us
a unique creation of God.
No two exactly alike.

We have this one thing in common—
we have a heart.
A heart which is the center
of our affections.
Our life style is in keeping with the love
which governs our heart.

If we are treasure centered,
we will strive,
and even plot and scheme,
to amass treasure.
When we are treasure centered,
our goal in life
will be to accumulate treasure.

And we will use our treasure in ways
that accord with
the desires of our heart.
If we are treasure centered,
there will not be strong scruples and guidelines
as to the way
in which we gain our treasure.

There will be dishonesty.
Not great lapses from the moral code,
but the little cheating and frauds

that cannot be detected,
but which we know in our heart are wrong.
There will be insensitivity
to the needs and concerns of others.
For where our treasure is,
there will our heart be also.

Treasure
can be a most possessive master.
Jesus said
in another pregnant saying,
"You cannot serve God and mammon."
You cannot serve the Lord of heaven and earth
when earthly goods
have become your god.

When we are God centered,
treasure is always gained and used
in keeping with the God who said,
"I am the Lord your God.
You shall have no other gods."

When we are God centered,
we will say those words,
we will hold those ideals,
we will practice those virtues
that are consonant
with the will of our God.

There will be honesty, integrity, charity.
There will be goodness, kindness, love.
There will be empathy, justice, and fairness to all.
There will be sensitivity
to the needs and concerns of every human being
and all creation.

Treasure
can lead us down blind alleys and dead end streets.
We become so intent upon the immediate gain
that we lose sight
of the long range goals of our God.

The role of treasure
in God's long range plan for us is seen
most truly
as we stand, as I stood this week,
at the mouth of the open tomb.
Treasure
cannot buy life
nor give life to the dead.
Our treasure cannot follow us into the life to come.

Treasure in Heaven

Treasure in heaven!
Jesus said,
"Sell your possessions and give to the poor.
Provide yourselves with purses
that do not grow old,
with a treasure in heaven that does not fail."

How many purses or wallets
have we had in our lifetime?
A purse that lasts an eternity has not been invented.
The life span of a purse is
a year or perhaps five years,
never a lifetime.
Purses are more mortal than we who carry them.

What is the treasure in heaven
of which Jesus spoke?
Will our gold and silver do?
No!
Earthly treasure is not transferable.
We pass from this life.
We are forever parted from our treasure here.

Jesus said,
"Where your heart is,
there will your treasure be also."
We are back to the heart!

Bread? or Crumbs?

The heart that pumps the blood
making sure that we live,
and breathe, and speak,
and act.
The heart!
The barometer of the goals and ideals
that issue from
our hands, our feet, our mouths, and our minds.

The heart is the key to all we are
and all we do.
Our heart determines our attitudes
and our relationship
to treasure and to people.
Above all, to people.

When treasure rules our heart,
we strive with all our strength to gain treasure.
Treasure is the measure of our life,
of our success in life.
Treasure is the goal for which we live.

When God rules our heart,
we strive with all our strength to do his will.
We become like God
in our loving deeds and in our loving words.
We become, as Luther said,
"Little Christs to one another."

The thoughts we think,
the attitudes we share,
the words we speak,
the deeds we do live after us,
enshrined in the minds and hearts of those
whose lives we touch day by day
as we walk the dusty road of life.

The treasure in heaven is
none other
than the loving thoughts,

Treasure and the Heart

the kindly words,
the beautiful deeds we have given
to those around us.

They live on forever,
always edifying, always strengthening,
always fulfilling
the lives of those around us,
as we reach out
to touch and to share with them the love and goodness
we have from God.

Treasure and the heart!
Entwined forever
in the lives of those of us in whose hearts abide
the spirit of him who said,
"Where your treasure is,
there will your heart be also."

24

Friend, Go Up Higher!

Luke 14.7–11

When he noticed how the guests chose the places of honor, he told them a parable. "When you are invited by someone to a wedding banquet, do not sit down at the place of honor, in case that someone more distinguished than you has been invited by your host; and the host who has invited both of you may come and say to you, 'Give this person your place,' and then in disgrace you would start to take the lower place. But when you are invited, go and sit at the lowest place, so that when your host comes, he may say to you, 'Friend, go up higher;' then you will be honored in the presence of all who sit at the table with you. For all who exalt themselves will be humbled, and those who humble themselves will be exalted."

Friend, Go up Higher!

An established custom in some churches,
especially in New England,
is the family pew.
A family rented a pew.
The pew was reserved
for the renting family only.
If a stranger entered
and occupied a rented pew,
that stranger was asked to go down lower,
to take another pew.

The Lower Seat

Jesus said,
"When you are invited,
do not sit in a seat of honor."
He noticed
how some tended to choose a seat of honor
at a banquet or party.
To choose the seat of honor can be
an embarrassment.

It could be that the seat
has been reserved for a guest of honor.
To be told publicly,
"Please take another seat"
can be most embarrassing.

What point was Jesus intending to make?
He was speaking on his favorite theme,
"The Kingdom of God."
There are those who believe
that seats at the right and at the left hand of God
should be reserved for them.

Two disciples,
James and John,
made such a request of Jesus.
They said,

Bread? or Crumbs?

"Let us sit at your right hand and at your left
when you come in your kingdom."

Jesus said,
"Those seats have been reserved
for someone special.
Moreover, the rental for those seats is very high.
Can you drink of my cup?
Will you be baptized with my baptism?"
The seats of honor
are reserved for those
who are totally committed to God.
Committed in the same measure
that Jesus was committed to his heavenly father.

Our custom in God's house is different.
Some of us believe
that the seats of honor are in the rear.
Whatever the reason,
it is universally common in Lutheran churches
to find the rear seats occupied
and the front pews vacant.

Our host in this place is God.
We treat God rather disdainfully, however.
We want to keep God at a distance.
Are we afraid of
a total commitment to God?
We all want his blessing,
but we want our commitment to be minimal.

It is true,
as Jesus said,
that the front seat before God
has a high cost—
a cup and a baptism.
That is, a total commitment
to our heavenly father.

Friend, Go Up Higher!

The Place of Honor

God is different from every human host or hostess.
We invite,
and we are invited,
because we expect to be invited in return.
Do we know a host or hostess
who invites those
who do not have the means to entertain in return?
A host who invites
the poor, the maimed,
the lame, and the blind?

Do we invite
the misfits, the outcasts,
the poorest members of our society?
These are the very ones God invites!
His invitation is inclusive.
He includes the poor,
the unworthy, the sinner, the outcast
in the invitation to his banquet.

Jesus went to people
whom the religious elite despised and rejected—
to tax collectors, sinners,
prodigals, and prostitutes.
He chose twelve to be his disciples.
Among them was a Judas who betrayed him
and a Peter who denied him.
He chose Paul,
a murderer and a persecutor.

God has never chosen the lily white
to sit at his banquet.
By his standards
we have all sinned and fallen beneath the level
of goodness and rightness.
Our ways of classifying people,
as was done at the Republican national convention recently,
is gross hypocrisy and wickedness.

Bread? or Crumbs?

There are no good people before God.
No one can claim the seat of honor.
Not a Moses, an Elijah,
a David, an Isaiah, a Peter, or a Paul.
Not even the brightest stars of the church—
St. Francis, Luther, Wesley,
or Billy Graham
can claim the seat next to God himself.

Strangely, however,
and contrary to everything I have said,
God has a seat of honor
for each one of us.
Not because we are deserving,
but because the Lord is good and gracious.

Behold the goodness of God!
We were lost, condemned,
hopelessly shackled by sin and wicked desires.
We have all gone our own way.
If God were human,
there would be no banquet.
There would be no one worthy to invite.

How gracious our God!
He sent his son with this invitation to all,
"Come, for all is now ready."
This is the gospel!
The message of our lesson today.
The invitation is from God himself,
and it is to you and to me.

God's invitation
has your name and my name written upon it.
There is a seat of honor
for each one of us
in the presence of God.
God has no stools in a corner
or a far off back pew.
There are only front pews for the people of God.

Friend, Go Up Higher!

When God speaks to us, he says,
"Friend, go up higher!"
We are at the bottom
of the great sea of humanity.
There is no way up,
not by our efforts or deserving.
The only way up is to hear God say,
"Friend, go up higher!"

That is what God is saying today.
God does not want us to remain afar off.
He does not want us to be undecided
or uncertain.
He wants us up front
to receive his blessing.
He wants to fill us with his good gifts and spirit.
He wants no one
to go empty away.

But there is a price
for this seat of honor.
There is a cup and there is a baptism.
The cup for Jesus
was self-denial and rejection.
The baptism
was suffering and death.

So it is for us.
There is a cup and a baptism.
A commitment,
a sacrifice, a sharing,
a forgiving, a praying,
a living and a dying for the God
whom we adore.

There is no seat of honor,
if we are unwilling to walk the way
Jesus walked.

Bread? or Crumbs?

There is a seat of honor for each one of us.
We are seated in God's pew
through his grace and mercy.
But God wants us to go up higher.

We are not yet what we are to be.
We are continually urged
by the word and by the Spirit of God
to go up higher.
To press on towards the goal of perfection
of which the apostle Paul spoke
in his letter to the Philippians.

Christians
who are unwilling to become more Christian
are always at risk.
We may strive to hold our seat
through our efforts and deserving.
This always ends in failure.

God always says to his own,
"Friend, go up higher."
Don't hedge and hesitate out of selfish concerns.
Don't labor under the false illusion
that the seat of honor
comes only at the end of this earthly life.
That seat is here and now
and only here and now for you and me.

God is a great God
and greatly to be praised.
Do not presume upon the goodness of God.
Do not hold the vain hope
that all will be well in the end.
Do not believe that a loving God
can never punish,
or reject, anyone in the end.

God's love is beyond human understanding.
The wonder is,

he invites even me.
The wonder is,
He bears with our weakness and our failures.
The glory of God is,
He says to you and to me,
"Friend, go up higher."

Be worthy of God.
Never treat God like a second cousin.
Proclaim his name
in every time and in every place.
Let your deeds and words
always honor the host
who has invited you.

Live as the people of God in this world.
A people
whom God has called out of darkness
into light.
A people
whom God has set free from the shackles of sin.
A people
who have power
to live godly and righteous lives
in the midst of those
who are cruel and false and wicked.

A people
who have the strength of God
to make the right decisions
about prejudice and jealousy and envy
and malice and hatred.
A people
who are empowered by God to love
the poor, the sinners,
the addicted,
those afflicted with the deadly aids virus.

A people
inspired by the spirit of God

to share our place of honor
with the least
and the most imperfect member of the human family.
A people
who rejoice in the privilege
to share the cup
of Jesus' self-denial and his rejection
by the elite
of the community.

A people
who are eager to share in Jesus' baptism—
in his suffering,
even in his death,
rather than to be unfaithful to God,
and to the trust
he has placed in us when he said,
"Friend, go up higher!"

25

Speak the Word!

Luke 7.1–10

After Jesus had finished all his sayings in the hearing of the people, he entered Capernaum. A centurion there had a slave whom he valued highly, and who was ill and close to death. When he heard about Jesus, he sent some Jewish elders to him, asking him to come and heal his slave. When they came to Jesus, they appealed to him earnestly, saying, "He is worthy of having you do this for him, for he loves our people, and it is he who built our synagogue for us. Jesus went with them, and when he was not far from the house, the centurion sent friends to say to him, "Lord, do not trouble yourself, for I am not worthy to have you come under my roof; therefore I did not presume to come to you. Only speak the word, and let my servant be healed. For I am also a man set under authority, with soldiers under me, and I say to one, 'Go,' and he goes, and to another, 'Come,' and he comes, and to my slave, 'Do this,' and the slave does it." When Jesus heard this he was amazed at him, and turning to the crowd that followed him, he said, "I tell you, not even in Israel have I found such faith." When those who had been sent returned to the house, they found the slave in good health.

Speak the Word!

The Word!
Powerful,
compelling in the mouth of one
with authority.
Our lesson focuses upon a man,
a Roman soldier,
an unusual man kindly and humane,
a man who loved his slave.
A man who loved the Jewish nation
over whom he exercised authority.

He sent Jewish friends
to Jesus
in behalf of his slave.
This man manifested
an unusual depth of humility
when he said,
"Lord, I am not worthy
to receive you under my roof.
Say the word
and my slave will be healed."

He was a good man,
humble, devout,
loving and caring,
a generous man
who had built a house of worship
for a people
of a different culture and religion
and of a different ethnic origin.

There was, however,
an area
over which this man exercised no authority.
His slave
was at the point of death.
He was helpless,
as we all are helpless,

Bread? or Crumbs?

when sickness threatens
the life of our beloved.

He could only appeal
to a higher authority
for help in his time of need.
The response to his plea was
the powerful word
of the one who said,
"Go;
let it be for you as you have believed."

This sickness unto death
is the sickness
that holds all in bondage
who know not the true God.
It was the sickness
that afflicted us
before we were baptized into Christ.

It is the sickness
that gives rise
to the many personal and social problems
that afflict the human family today—
racism,
sexism,
abuse,
addiction,
prejudice,
selfishness,
pride,
and self-righteousness
to mention only a few.

We are helpless,
as the Roman soldier was helpless,
in the presence
of this sickness unto death.

Speak the Word!

There is one
who comes from God
with the powerful word of release,
the one whom God has sent
to deliver us
and all creation
from bondage
to this sickness unto death.

We who have been delivered,
we who have been marked
with the cross of Christ,
are free.
Free to love
with a love
that transcends every barrier
of status,
race,
or religion.

Free to love
those in bondage,
the helpless,
the dispossessed,
the ugly,
the mean,
the wicked,
the cruel,
the boasters,
the fanatics.

Free to love
those who would rob us
of our personhood
and bring us into subjection
to their purpose and will.

There is a word,
a word from God,
which we have in our hearts

and on our lips.
A word
of peace and hope and joy.
A word
that has changed
our selfish, inordinate self-love
into a passion for all those afflicted
by the sickness unto death.

We have been empowered
by the word of the living God
to do what Jesus did,
to speak the word
that breaks down every barrier
separating us from one another.

A word
that can shape and mold
all humanity
into one family
where there is neither
Asian nor American,
black nor white,
male nor female.

This is our calling.
This is why we wear
the name of Christ.
To speak
the powerful word of the gospel
to all who are at the point of death.

We come as the Roman soldier,
helpless and inadequate,
to the one who has said,
"All authority
has been given to me
in heaven and on earth.
Go!"

26

A Man Had Died

Luke 7.11–17

Soon afterwards he went to a town called Nain, and his disciples and a large crowd went with him. As he approached the gate of the town, a man who had died was being carried out. He was his mother's only son, and she was a widow; and with her was a large crowd from the town. When the Lord saw her, he had compassion for her and said to her, "Do not weep." Then he came forward and touched the bier, and the bearers stood still. He said, "Young man, I say to you, Rise!" The dead man sat up and began to speak, and Jesus gave him to his mother. Fear seized all of them; and they glorified God, saying, "A great prophet has risen among us!" and "God has looked favorably on his people!" This word about him spread throughout Judea and all the surrounding country.

A Man Had Died

A young man had died,
the only son
of a widow.
This is not an unusual story.
The daily obituaries
inform us
of the frequency of these events.

Death is always tragic,
especially for the young
who have so much to live for.
The death
of this young man
was especially tragic,
since his mother depended upon him
to provide her
with the necessities of life.

There was weeping
and wailing.
There was not even the lively hope
of resurrection to life
with God.
A man descended
to Sheol,
a dark and shadowy place
with no real existence.

The real tragedy of death
is most often for those
who are left behind.
This is what makes this story
so pathetic.
There was weeping and wailing.
The weeping and wailing continues
for days,
and weeks,
and years.

Bread? or Crumbs?

We know of parents
who have left their son's room
as it was
the day he died.
They relive their sorrow daily.
What can we say to help?
Can we,
like Jesus,
stop the funeral procession
and say,
"Young man, arise?"

Most often
we can only join
the sad procession
and add our tears
to those shed by the mourners.

Our story ends
on a happy note.
Jesus stopped the procession.
He said,
"Young man, arise."
He sat up
and began to speak.

How dramatic!
How marvelous!
Imagine the joy of this mother
at the restoration of her son.
Death
was overcome
with a word from the one
who had come from God.
If only Jesus were here
when our dear one has died.

Our problem is
our attention to the physical.

A Man Had Died

Jesus did not come from God
to bring an end
to physical death.

He came
to overcome our bondage
to the death of the spirit.
Death
of the spirit
is one of that dread trinity
to which we and all humanity
are subject.

The Apostle
describes our situation
in these descriptive words,
"We were dead
in our trespasses and sins."

This story
is intended to proclaim
the good news
that God has come in Jesus
to deliver us
from all that separates us
from God,
especially our bondage
to a dead spirit.

We are the living dead
until Jesus comes
to touch us,
to speak the word,
"Young man,
young woman,
I say to you, arise!"

We are the living dead
even though we breathe
and move

and take nourishment.
To be alive is
to be alive in God!

To know that each moment,
each day,
each year,
is a precious gift of his grace.
To know
that our life counts
as we use every opportunity
God gives to make an impact
for good,
for truth,
and for love
upon the lives of those about us.

The call of God is to life!
To have a dimension
of meaning
for all that we are and do.
Not to be the victim of sin,
or selfishness,
or meaninglessness.

That is the way
God would have it for us.
We were dead,
but we are alive by his grace.

We have the rare privilege
of sharing
this testimony with others.
A man was dead,
but he is alive,
touched by the hand
of the living God!

This is the eternal gospel of God.
This is the story

A Man Had Died

of your life and mine,
for the young man in our lesson is
YOU!
He is I!
Behold, we were dead,
but we are alive forevermore!

27

The Least and the Greater

Matthew 11.2–19

When John heard in prison what the Messiah was doing, he sent word by his disciples and said to him, "Are you the one who is to come, or are we to wait for another?" Jesus answered them, "Go and tell John what you hear and see; the blind receive their sight, the lame walk, the lepers are cleansed, the deaf hear, the dead are raised, and the poor have good news brought to them. And blessed is anyone who takes no offense at me."

As they went away, Jesus began to speak to the crowds about John: "What did you go out into the wilderness to look at? A reed shaken by the wind? What then did you go out to see? Someone dressed in soft robes? Look, those who wear soft robes are in royal palaces. What then did you go out to see? A prophet? Yes, I tell you, and more than a prophet. This is the one about whom it is written,
'See, I am sending my messenger
ahead of you,
who will prepare your way
before you.'
Truly I tell you, among those born of women no one has arisen greater than John the Baptist; yet the least in the kingdom of heaven is greater than he. From the days of John the Baptist until now the kingdom of heaven has suffered violence, and the violent take it by force. For all the prophets and the law prophesied until John came, and if you are willing to accept it, he is Elijah who is to come. Let anyone with ears listen!

But to what will I compare this generation? It is like children sitting in the marketplaces and calling to one another,
'We played the flute for you,
and you did not dance;

We wailed, and you did not mourn.'
John came neither eating nor drinking and they say, 'He has a demon;' the Son of Man came eating and drinking, and they say, 'Look a glutton and a drunkard, a friend of tax collectors and sinners!' Yet wisdom is vindicated by her deeds."

The Least and the Greater

The faith history
of the human family
has been fashioned
by a few decisive persons.
Jesus pointed to John the baptizer
as one.

He said,
"Among those born of woman
there is no one greater than John."
Yet John
according to our view is
only a footnote to history.

We do not study his theology,
nor emulate his life style,
nor adore him
as a leading saint of the church.
We do not even administer baptism
according to his style.

John was an innovator,
who broke with tradition,
who reinterpreted scripture
and instituted a baptism that became
a prototype
for Christian usage.
John is mentioned more often
than any other person
in the gospels
after Jesus.

Evidently Jesus held John
in high regard.
His testimony to John is
high praise.
Then he added these words,
"The least person

in the kingdom of God
is greater than John."

He said this to the crowds
who gathered
to hear his teaching.
To whom did he refer?
Surely not to every person
before him,
but only to that person
who is "in the kingdom."

The identity of this least person
must be determined
by a study of Jesus' sayings;
such as,
"Not everyone who says to me
'Lord, Lord,'
will enter
the kingdom of heaven,
but *only* the one
who does the will of my Father."

Doing the will of God is basic.
Doing the will of God
can only issue
from an honest and good heart,
for Jesus said,
"First make the tree good
and then its fruit will be good."

Doing the will of God is
the spontaneous expression
of the one
whose heart and life are
in accord with God.

Jesus refers
to you and to me.
We cannot claim greatness

The Least and the Greater

for ourselves,
since few of us are exemplary persons,
nor are we innovators
and decisive persons
when compared
to John the baptizer.

Nonetheless Jesus said,
"The least person
in the kingdom of heaven
is greater than John."
How can this be?

This is the reality
because we live on this side
of the cross.
John belonged to the time
of preparation
for the salvation event
that was only realized
when Jesus spoke those pregnant words
from the cross,
"It is finished!"

We belong
to the age of salvation,
for we have been baptized
into the death and resurrection
of Christ.
We are great in privilege
and in opportunity,
for we are empowered
by the Spirit of God
to know the mind of God
in a way not possible for John,
and to have the high privilege
of doing
the will of God here and now.

Bread? or Crumbs?

We are the least in the kingdom.
Yet by God's grace
we are the greatest.
This is not an invitation
from our Lord
to be proud,
or to lord it over anyone,
but rather to become
in the words of our Lord,
"The servant of all."

We are the hands
consecrated by God
to minister to the sick
and to the dying,
to feed the hungry
and to clothe the naked,
to cleanse the wounds
of anger
and passion
that we inflict upon one another.

We are the feet
consecrated
to carry the good news
of the gospel
to every person
who knows not God.

We are the mouths
consecrated
to speak his word
of acceptance and forgiveness
to the wayward and the fallen.

We are the hearts
consecrated
to love without reservation
those of a different life style
and of a different cultural and ethnic origin.

The Least and the Greater

We are the minds
consecrated
to truth,
justice,
and equality for all.
Our Lord says to you and to me,
"You, the least are the greatest of all.
Blessed are you
when you do these things."

28

The Alabaster Flask

Luke 7.36–50

One of the Pharisees asked Jesus to eat with him, and he went into the Pharisee's house and took his place at the table. And a woman in the city, who was a sinner, having learned that he was eating in the Pharisee's house, brought an alabaster jar of ointment. She stood behind him at his feet, weeping, and began to bathe his feet with her tears and to dry them with her hair. Then she began kissing his feet and anointing them with the ointment. Now when the Pharisee who had invited him saw it, he said to himself, "If this man were a prophet, he would have known who and what kind of woman this is who is touching him—that she is a sinner." Jesus spoke up and said to him, "Simon, I have somethng to say to you." "Teacher," he replied, "Speak!" "A certain creditor had two debtors; one owed five hundred denarii, and the other fifty. When they could not pay, he cancelled the debts for both of them. Now which of them will love him more?" Simon answered, "I suppose, the one for whom he canceled the greater debt." Jesus said to him, "You have judgeded rightly." Then turning toward the woman, he said to Simon, "Do you see this woman? I entered your house; you gave me no water for my feet, but she has bathed my feet with her tears and dried them with her hair. You gave me no kiss, but from the time I came in she has not stopped kissing my feet. You did not anoint my head with oil, but she has anointed my feet with ointment. Therefore, I tell you, her sins, which were many, have been forgiven; hence she has shown great love. But to the one to whom little is forgiven loves little." Then he said to her, "Your sins are forgiven." But those who were at table with him began to say among themselves, "Who is this who even forgives sins?" And he said to the woman, "Your faith has saved you; go in peace."

The Alabaster Flask

Alabaster!
A carbonate of lime
used in ancient times
to make ointment vases.
A beautiful banded mineral
that carved easily
and polished beautifully,
sometimes used for adorning homes
and public buildings.

How marvelously
God has put all the world together
in a harmony,
in a glory and beauty
beyond our ingenuity to reproduce.

What are humans
to have been given power and dominion
over all God has made?
The ability
to extract alabaster from nature,
to carve and shape it
into beautiful shapes and patterns,
a delight to the eye
and to the touch?

Humans—
the crown of all that God has made;
yet shaped of the same atoms
of which the alabaster vase is composed.

There was a human,
a woman of the city
who came with her alabaster flask of ointment,
a woman
of poor reputation,
a sinner.

Bread? or Crumbs?

She came not to partake of bread,
but to share her grief,
her tears,
and her ointment
with the guest of the house.

There was the host,
rich, urbane,
a religious man,
a man in love with himself
who saw no sins
in his doing.
A critical, fault-finding man,
who even despised his guest
for his lack of discernment
concerning this woman.

The woman in our story
a sinner.
Simon,
the Pharisee,
a righteous man in his own eyes.

Sinners are readily known
by their deeds;
deeds hardly hidden
from the scrutinizing eyes
of the righteous.

Which of the two mirrors our self?
Are we the ones
who come in grief and in tears
with our alabaster flask of ointment?
Or are we the ones
who judge and condemn
those who do not meet the standards
of our life style?

What was the sin of the woman?
We are not told.

The Alabaster Flask

What was Simon's sin?
Pride,
that deadly sin
that has no forgiveness.
For those who carry this sin
have no grief,
no tears,
no alabaster flask of ointment
to bring to God.

There is another in our story,
a man whose feet were wet
with the hot tears
of this sinful woman.
A patient, compassionate man
who takes the sins,
the anguish of this sinful woman
upon himself.

How gently he deals with her
and even with proud, sinless Simon.
He says to her,
"Your sins are forgiven."

This is the gospel!
The good news
that God delivers us
and every sinner
from the guilt and penalty of our fault.

Forgiveness
not granted
because it is the business of God to forgive,
not because we come with our tears,
our cries,
our alabaster flask of ointment,
but only because God has sent One
to take our sin,
our guilt,
our punishment upon himself.

Bread? or Crumbs?

The lesson—
we are not,
we cannot be,
right before God
apart from his gracious forgiveness.
We are not,
we cannot be,
right with one another
apart from God's gracious forgiveness.

Forgiveness
comes with great cost.
God gave his own Son
to cruel death
to gain our release.
Forgivness
is that great renewing stream
that cleanses our hearts,
our minds,
and our lives from every stain.

We are forgiven by God's grace
that we may be forgiving
and loving
even to the worst of sinners,
especially forgiving
to those who labor
under the heavy sin of pride
and self-righteousness.

How splendid
that our egos are renewed
and made whole
by the gracious gift of forgiveness.
Fashioned
out of the dust of the ground
to be more than an alabaster flask.

The Alabaster Flask

Fashioned in the image
of our Creator God
to show forth his glory
by loving all that he has made;
and by forgiving
all whose humanity
is manifested
in their dark attitudes,
in their unworthy deeds,
and in their harsh and cruel words.

Forgiving,
for we too
are fashioned of the same alabaster
with the same
harsh and cruel attitudes, deeds,
and words.
Forgiving,
for we too have been forgiven
by the one who said
to this woman
with her alabaster flask,
"Your sins are forgiven."

www.ingramcontent.com/pod-product-compliance
Lightning Source LLC
Chambersburg PA
CBHW071147300426
44113CB00009B/1110